PRESENTED TO:

_____

FROM:

_____

Sleep
ON THIS

EVENING REFLECTIONS
FROM GOD'S WORD

DR. DAVID JEREMIAH

Turning Point
with Dr. David Jeremiah

ISBN: [978-1-951701-34-5]
ISBN: [978-1-951701-40-6] eBook

Created and Produced for Turning Point Ministries by
Breakfast for Seven
2150 E. Continental Blvd., Southlake, TX 76092

Printed in China.

CONTENTS

HOW TO USE THIS DEVOTIONAL

Each of these one hundred Scriptures and brief reflections should be read right before you close your eyes for sleep. As you prepare for bed, begin to direct your heart expectantly toward your Father.

Ideally, you'll have a small reading light on your bedside table so you can read the entry from bed with all other lights out. Read the Scripture and reflection *out loud* if you are able.

When finished, turn off the light, close your eyes, and invite the Holy Spirit to continue to minister these concepts to your spirit and soul as you sleep. With a heart full of gratitude, simply continue to meditate upon what you've just read and heard.

Prepare to start your journey into sweeter sleep tonight.

Introduction

Sleep. It's a bit of a mystery. Scientists still aren't completely sure why we need it. But we clearly do.

A growing mountain of research reveals that the quality of our sleep has a major impact on every aspect of our health and well-being. The evidence continues to mount—good sleep promotes feeling better in body, mind, and soul.

Our Eternal God watches over us. He never slumbers, He never sleeps, and He desires to give us the rest He created us to need.

Describing the benefits of getting wisdom, Proverbs 3:24 says:

> *When you lie down, you will not be afraid;*
> *when you lie down, your sleep will be sweet* (NIV).

And note these promises from Psalms:

> *In peace I will lie down and sleep,*
> *for you alone, Lord, make me dwell in safety.*
> Psalm 4:8, NIV

He grants sleep to those he loves.
Psalm 127:2, NIV

Clearly, God cares about our sleep! And His Word contains truths that help us get a refreshing, renewing, restorative night's sleep. Yet far too often, we drift off to sleep with our head and heart filled with worry—our mind swirling with anxiety over the challenges we know we will face in the day ahead or our mind replaying a distressing conversation or confrontation we had earlier.

This certainly isn't the wise way to prepare to go to sleep. On the contrary, it's a prescription for fitful dreams and tormented tossing and turning.

Over the years I've learned the power of starting my day the night before. I've discovered that if I do that, the following day goes much better. And this devotional is designed to help you do the same, to provide your heart and mind with biblical truth and encouragement for refreshing rest in "the night watches."

When I remember You on my bed,
I meditate on You in the night watches.
Psalm 63:7, NASB

**HOW TO USE THE QR CODES
THROUGHOUT *SLEEP ON THIS*:**

Step 1: Open the camera app on your phone.

Step 2: Move your phone until the QR code is in focus. On some devices, you might have to fit the QR code inside the square that will pop up on your screen.

Step 3: You should automatically be redirected to the URL connected with the QR code. If not, the link to the website should pop up on your screen, and you will need to click on it.

If you are having trouble getting the QR code to scan through your camera, try checking the different camera modes your phone offers—it's possible you will need to switch modes and try again.

Special Note: *Each QR code will direct you to a different URL, so be sure to scan each day's code.*

—*1*—

In the Night
WATCHES

When I remember You on my bed, I meditate on You in the night watches. Because You have been my help, therefore in the shadow of Your wings I will rejoice. My soul follows close behind You; Your right hand upholds me.

PSALM 63:6-8

LISTEN

The psalmist King David was not someone who tossed and turned in the night, worrying over things that were beyond his control. Even though the circumstances he faced as he composed the sixty-third psalm were quite dire.

When insomnia drove sleep from his eyes, David knew one sure remedy. He would meditate upon God.

Have you ever had a problem so troublesome that you've lost sleep over it? We all have. What did David do when this happened? He remembered God upon his bed. He meditated on Him in the night watches.

Take a cue from the man after God's own heart (1 Samuel 13:14). Meditate on God and recall all the help He has given you and blessings He has bestowed upon you in the past.

Sleep on This:

Turn your thoughts from your problems to your God. He is your help. Rejoice in the shadow of His wings.

No Goodbyes
IN HEAVEN

*And God will wipe away every tear from their eyes; there
shall be no more death, nor sorrow, nor crying. There shall
be no more pain, for the former things have passed away.*

REVELATION 21:4

LISTEN

*G*oodbyes are often painful. We all have precious loved ones who have moved out of our lives—many who have moved on to heaven. But with the authority of the Word of God and the resurrection of Jesus Christ, I want to reassure you that heaven is a place where we'll never say goodbye. The Bible says that heaven is our eternal home.

The apostle Paul exhorts us not to "sorrow as others who have no hope. For if we believe that Jesus died and rose again, even so God will bring with Him those who sleep in Jesus.... And thus we shall always be with the Lord" (1 Thessalonians 4:13-14, 17).

Sleep on This:

As it relates to your loved ones in Christ, your goodbyes will become hellos, your separation will turn into reunion, and your fellowship will never cease. Someone once said, "Unbelievers only meet to part again; Christians only part to meet again." In heaven, we'll never have to say a final goodbye to anyone.

— 3 —

No Place

FOR FEAR

The Lord is on my side; I will not fear.

PSALM 118:6

LISTEN

*W*ould you store your food processor in your clothes dryer? Of course not. The food processor would disrupt your routines. You would have to remove it when it came time to dry your clothes. That's the value of having a proper place for everything.

So why would you store fear in your heart? It can do nothing except get in the way of what God wants to do in your life. Fear is not part of the fruit of the Spirit found in Galatians 5:22-23. Think about how out of place fear looks in this list: love, joy, peace, longsuffering, FEAR, kindness, goodness, faithfulness, gentleness, self-control. Fear is most definitely out of place in the believer's heart.

Our plan of action is resistance: "Resist the devil and he will flee from you" (James 4:7). We resist, deny, set aside, and choose not to embrace what we know is not of God. Let's agree with the psalmist in tonight's key verse. Because "the Lord is on my side; I will not fear."

Sleep on This:

The Lord is with you. He is for you. He loves you. And greater is He "who is in you… than he who is in the world" (1 John 4:4), so there is no place in your heart for fear.

God Is Faithful

*God is faithful, by whom you were called into the
fellowship of His Son, Jesus Christ our Lord.*

1 CORINTHIANS 1:9

LISTEN

*F*or fallible humans like you and me, promises are easier to make than to keep. For better or worse, our faithfulness reflects our personal integrity for keeping whatever promises we have made. Here's some good news: Human integrity is simply a pale reflection of the impeccable and infallible faithfulness of God.

To us, this is one of His most cherished attributes because it means that everything about Him is reliable. Your Heavenly Father's faithfulness springs from His divine determination to do as He has said. Always. And without variance. Because of that faithfulness, you can lie down tonight in total confidence in every promise in His Word. You can rest in complete freedom from anxiety and worry.

Sleep on This:

When you understand God's essential nature, you then know you have a secure basis for rest and peace in Him. He can be trusted to keep His promises. When you open the covers of His Word, you're opening a lockbox of promissory notes that are backed by the full faith and credit of heaven.

Always Working

*And we know that all things work together for good
to those who love God, to those who are the called
according to His purpose. For whom He foreknew, He
also predestined to be conformed to the image of His Son,
that He might be the firstborn among many brethren.*

ROMANS 8:28-29

LISTEN

One of the most comforting truths in the Bible is that the sovereign providence of God extends to the daily details of our life. He isn't just concerned about the nations, but about the sparrows, the lilies—and me and you. His control extends over all our days and all our ways, and He is able to work all things together for our good.

We don't have a God who takes vacations. He is always watching. Always working.

So when you read frightening headlines, when you face disappointing setbacks and adversity in life, when your world seems to be coming apart and you aren't sure what's going on, remember—God is sovereign.

Sleep on This:

As you lie down to rest, take comfort in the knowledge that God is in control. Find peace in the knowledge that He works all things for His glory and for your good.

— *6* —

Present,
NOT DISTANT

All the way around shall be eighteen thousand cubits;
and the name of the city from that day shall be:
THE LORD IS THERE.

EZEKIEL 48:35

LISTEN

*I*n the latter chapters of Ezekiel, God gave him some of the most incredible prophecies found in the Bible. The Lord told him of a day when Jerusalem would be restored. And that city—the future millennial capital of Jerusalem—would have a nickname. It would be known in Hebrew as Jehovah-Shammah—"The-Lord-Is-There."

When you pray, you can address your Heavenly Father as Jehovah-Shammah. Try it tonight as you close your eyes to rest. He is there, near you, with you, ever present. When you pray, your words don't have to travel millions of miles into space to reach God. He is in the same room with you, as close as your own spirit, closer than a brother. He is your Jehovah-Shammah.

Sleep on This:

The God you love and who loves you is not distant. There is nowhere you can go where He isn't present. Right now, in this quiet moment and all through the night, He is "The-Lord-[Who]-Is-There."

—7—

Putting Fear
IN ITS PLACE

*There is no fear in love; but perfect love casts out
fear, because fear involves torment. But he who
fears has not been made perfect in love.*

1 JOHN 4:18

LISTEN

*N*o doubt you recall the children's fable "The Three Little Pigs." A ravenous wolf appeared on each of the three pigs' doorsteps, and the first two pigs fled in fear to the third pig's house. But the third little pig was prepared because he was surrounded by a house much stronger than the wolf's hot air threats. Inside the house of brick, the three pigs were safe. They were composed, calm, and confident. They knew that their enemy had no power to destroy them as long as they were protected by the strong walls of the brick house.

We never know when fear is going to come knocking—or pounding!—on our door. Fear may be demanding that you open the door of your heart today. If not today, it will happen another day. So we need to be prepared. We need to know how to put fear in its place and keep it there until all danger has passed. How?

Living by faith keeps fear in its place. And faith grows when you contemplate God's immense love for you.

Sleep on This:

You are loved by a Heavenly Father who, according to 1 John 4:8 and 16, "is love." That love is a fortress that surrounds you tonight and every night.

— 8 —

Lay Your
BURDENS DOWN

*And He said, "My Presence will go with
you, and I will give you rest."*

EXODUS 33:14

LISTEN

*I*n Exodus 33:14, the Lord told Moses, "My Presence will go with you, and I will give you rest." He says the same to you tonight. You can rest in His promises, rest in His sovereignty, rest in His love, rest in His grace, and rest in His ability to deliver you from all your fears.

The rest you need isn't a cessation of activity. It is the calming of anxiety. It's the inner tranquility that allows you to be still and know Him.

Tonight, you can rest in who He is, in what He is like, and in all He can do. Come to Him and lay down your heavy burdens. Let Him give you rest.

Sleep on This:

Jesus doesn't intend or require that you carry heavy burdens. His will is not drudgery. His plans for you are good. Are you trying to carry things you shouldn't? Cares, worries, or fears? Lay them down. And rest.

Encourage
YOURSELF

But David strengthened himself in the Lord his God.

1 SAMUEL 30:6

LISTEN

*D*avid, the shepherd-king, once found himself in a deep hole of despair in the village of Ziklag. His mentor, Samuel, was dead. David had been rejected and denied safety by the Philistines. The Amalekites had invaded his camp and kidnapped his family and his men's families. His friends were turning on him, and his loyal band of followers was ready to stone him. Saddest of all, his dear friend Jonathan was unable to come to him.

In David's dark moment, we encounter a powerful sentence in God's Word. It is tonight's key verse. And it reveals one of our most vital spiritual techniques. Call it self-encouragement. Or call it PTL (Praise the Lord) therapy. When our family and friends aren't with us, when we're between a rock and a hard place, when we're in Ziklag, we've got to know how to strengthen ourselves in the Lord by spending time in prayer and worship and meditating on the promises in God's Word.

Sleep on This:

The darkness of the bedroom can feel like a lonely place—even when you share a bed with a spouse. But you are not alone. And like David, you can encourage yourself "in the Lord" right now.

Live in the Calm

But He said to them, "Why are you fearful, O you of little faith?" Then He arose and rebuked the winds and the sea, and there was a great calm.

MATTHEW 8:26

LISTEN

God can keep us calm amid any danger. Sometimes we're caught in plagues and pandemics that sweep over our land. Other times, we're caught in problems and perplexities that are targeted exclusively at us.

But, my friend, the Lord's calming presence gives us strength. Live in that calm. Choose to live in a fearless state of mind. Learn what the Bible says about calmness; actively worship when you're tempted to worry; claim God's calming verses; change the way you think one incident at a time; surrender every situation to Him.

Remember, when you are in Christ, it is well with your soul.

Sleep on This:

No matter what kind of storm you may be facing tonight, allow the Lord's calming presence to give you strength and peace.

Take the Fourth

OPTION

For God has not given us a spirit of fear,
but of power and of love and of a sound mind.

2 TIMOTHY 1:7

LISTEN

*D*efining fear is not hard. It's an emotion. One that is actually the result of waves of chemicals that flow through your body when you encounter a perceived threat—whether real or imagined. That response is the well-known "fight, flight, or freeze" response.

I have good news for you. There is a fourth "f" option —faith!

When you encounter a real threat or when the enemy of your soul whispers to you about a possible threat in your future, you can either run, try to fight, remain paralyzed with fear, or take the fourth option: Put fear in its place by faith.

When you feel afraid, it's time to recognize the feeling for what it is and respond with faith. We put fear in its place with faith that is built on God's Word and past experiences with God's faithfulness.

Sleep on This:

God has given you a spirit "of power and of love and of a sound mind." That means you don't have to succumb to fear. Ponder God's promises and His lovingkindness—and choose faith instead.

—12—

Rest Assured

Blessed be the God and Father of our Lord Jesus Christ, who according to His abundant mercy has begotten us again to a living hope through the resurrection of Jesus Christ from the dead.

1 PETER 1:3

LISTEN

*H*ave you ever paused to consider how much of our life is spent trying to stave off fears and worries? We go to enormous lengths trying to find security, trying to find a way of protecting our futures, our homes, our property, our retirement, our finances, our families, and our identities.

There are things in life we can't control or even successfully manage. If we aren't careful, we can get caught in the trap of self-sufficiency. We live in an uncertain world, and no lasting security is ever found by relying on the things of this life.

As Christians, we can live in absolute security because of one game-changing event in history—the resurrection of Jesus Christ. This is a "living hope" that, when properly viewed, outweighs any and every earthly fear.

Sleep on This:

As you close your eyes, ponder this biblical truth that puts every fear in perspective. As a born-again believer, you are going to live forever. Because Jesus was raised from the dead, you can rest assured that you will spend eternity with Him.

—13—

Peace

IN HIS PRESENCE

The Lord will give strength to His people;
the Lord will bless His people with peace.

PSALM 29:11

LISTEN

*P*rayer is our primary method for telling Jesus about our worries and, in the process, recognizing the presence of God. We draw near to Him in prayer, and in His presence is peace, comfort, and assurance. Admittedly, this may take some time. It often takes a season of abiding in the Lord before our heart breaks through into the fullness of His peace. That's where perseverance and patience come in.

Sometimes peace comes instantly; other times it comes slowly but surely as we linger before God's throne. In either case, our fear level is, in a way, an indicator of the current closeness of our friendship with God. Closer means calmer. And we grow stronger as we learn to cast our cares on Him in prayer.

Sleep on This:

Close your day with prayer. Tell the Father about your concerns and worries. As you do, know that He will bless you with peace.

You're Enough

BECAUSE HE IS ENOUGH

Not that we are sufficient of ourselves to think of anything as being from ourselves, but our sufficiency is from God, who also made us sufficient as ministers of the new covenant, not of the letter but of the Spirit; for the letter kills, but the Spirit gives life.

2 CORINTHIANS 3:5-6

LISTEN

$\mathcal{W}$e all need affirmation. As a result, the quest to be affirmed by others can often become an insatiable craving. Ubiquitous social media with its accompanying "likes" and "loves" can turn this craving into a daily obsession.

Here is the antidote for this malady. Recognize that your Heavenly Father has already affirmed you. God chose you and drew you to Himself. In Jesus Christ you are free to love others unconditionally.

Jesus is more than enough. His grace is sufficient. His love and acceptance are all we need.

Sleep on This:

As tonight's key verse reminds us, none of us are sufficient in ourselves. But in God we are completely and totally sufficient. You are enough because He is enough.

— 15 —

Take Shelter Here

He who dwells in the secret place of the Most High
shall abide under the shadow of the Almighty.

PSALM 91:1

LISTEN

*T*hink about the name "Almighty" in this evening's key verse. We do not have a weak God. Our God cannot grow weary; He cannot misunderstand or mislead. He cannot fail. His might is all around us. It is all-inclusive. And it works all for the best.

Why is this important? Because our anxiety fades in proportion to our awareness of the Almighty and His care for us. We cannot have an all-powerful God and at the same time have an unsolvable problem. We can have one or the other, but not both.

Tonight, take your fear—all your foreboding and anxious care—and give it to the Almighty, under whose shadow you find shelter.

Sleep on This:

The Almighty knows how to protect you amid protracted situations. He has ample power over your panic, and He can replace your discouragement with determination to count it all joy. Find deep rest in the "secret place" of His care tonight.

— *16* —

He Knows

WHAT YOU DON'T

*Behold, God is my salvation, I will trust and not
be afraid; "For Yah, the Lord, is my strength and
song; He also has become my salvation."*

ISAIAH 12:2

LISTEN

Stress. It's common in our culture and too much, too consistently is unhealthy. We all know that. If I had to boil the very large discussion of stress down to one simple definition, it would be this: Stress is fear of the unknown.

I'm talking about the kind of stress that rapidly develops into fear: When will this end? How will it end? What will be the cost of this circumstance? How will it look to others if I fail? Stress is looking into the future—whether an hour, a day, a week, a month, or a year—and seeing nothing but a huge question mark on the horizon.

If you want to live a stress free life, you need to live a life of trust. Trust in God's faithfulness, goodness, power, and might.

Sleep on This:

Psalm 56:3 says, "Whenever I am afraid, I will trust in You." Disarm stress by addressing the fears behind it. God is your salvation. Let your heart trust in Him. You don't have to fear the unknown because the God who loves you knows all things.

Turn Agitation

INTO EXPECTATION

My soul, wait silently for God alone,
for my expectation is from Him.

PSALM 62:5

LISTEN

*P*lacing our faith in God does more than just console us. It creates expectancy. Put another way, it sends a positive force into our heart to strengthen us. Suddenly, we expect the Lord to work, to move, to do what only He can do.

What kind of expectation does faith produce? Not that God will do exactly what we think or want, but that He will do what's ultimately best for us from His perspective in eternity. Our fearful circumstance may seem like a tangled knot to us, but our Lord knows how to unravel the complexities and untangle the perplexities.

Faith turns agitation into expectation. And our expectation is an acclamation that our sovereign Heavenly Father can do what we cannot.

Sleep on This:

Put your faith and trust in your sovereign Heavenly Father tonight. As you do, expect Him to work out your circumstances for your good. Expect that He can and will untangle even your most complex problems.

— 18 —

Both Known

AND LOVED

Great is our Lord, and mighty in power;
His understanding is infinite.

PSALM 147:5

LISTEN

*O*ur Heavenly Father's understanding has no limits or boundaries. That means His knowledge of our situations is limitless too. His attention is on you. God knows where you are at every moment (Psalm 139:7-12). He knows everything about you (Psalm 139:13-15). He knows every moment of your future (Psalm 139:16). He knows how you will respond in each circumstance.

God knows when every bird falls from the sky and knows the number of hairs on your head (Luke 12:6-7). He knows what you need—food, clothing, and the like—for your life and has promised to provide (Matthew 6:25-34). How can God give that kind of attention to more than seven billion people on planet Earth? Because of who He is—infinite in His being (1 Kings 8:27) and omniscient in His knowledge.

Sleep on This:

Here's wonderful news: God's infinite power and knowledge are coupled with His compassion. This means God *can* not only give you His attention, but He *wants* to do so! God not only knows you, He also loves you.

Sure-Footed

IN A TIME OF TROUBLE

The Lord God is my strength; He will make my feet like
deer's feet, and He will make me walk on my high hills.

HABAKKUK 3:19

LISTEN

As we come to understand more of God's character and faithfulness, we can begin underlining His Word. That is, we can go into the Bible and locate promises designed to meet our current needs.

Many Christians are familiar with the most quoted promises about God working all things for our good (Romans 8:28), directing our paths (Proverbs 3:5-6), and supplying all our needs out of the riches of His glory (Philippians 4:19). But there are hundreds of other truths, assurances, and comforts in the Bible. Tonight's key verse is one of them.

This verse deserves to be underlined and pondered. No matter how precarious your current position may seem, God will make sure you overcome it safely and securely.

Sleep on This:

You're not expected to manage your current or future circumstances in your own strength. The Lord God is your strength. And He is able to keep your feet secure, even as you navigate the "high hills" of life.

— 20 —

Knowing

AND BEING KNOWN

*I am the good shepherd; and I know My sheep, and am
known by My own. As the Father knows Me, even so I
know the Father; and I lay down My life for the sheep.*

JOHN 10:14-15

LISTEN

*Y*ou have your Savior's undivided attention. Did you know that?

In tonight's key verse, Jesus reminds us that He knows us and laid down His life for us. He also highlights the kind of relationship He had (and has) with the Father. That kind of father-son mutual attentiveness is a picture of what should be true of God and His human sons and daughters. More than any of the four Gospel writers, the apostle John focused on the intimacy between the Father and the Son as captured in Jesus' own words.

That same intimacy is available to you in Jesus. Be reminded tonight that Jesus is the Good Shepherd. He knows you and invites you to know the Father as He does.

Sleep on This:

Jesus, the Good Shepherd, laid down His life for you. You have His undivided attention. And in Him you have been invited into a relationship with the Father in which you can know Him, just as He knows and loves you.

21

He Is

IN YOUR TOMORROW

Therefore do not worry about tomorrow, for tomorrow will worry about its own things. Sufficient for the day is its own trouble.

MATTHEW 6:34

LISTEN

*T*onight's key verse comes at the end of a long string of our Lord's "Do not worry" statements: "Therefore I say to you, do not worry.... Which of you by worrying.... So why do you worry.... Therefore do not worry.... Therefore do not worry" (Matthew 6:25-34).

Perhaps Jesus was keenly aware of His disciples'—and our own—tendency to worry. In a similar vein, James told us, "You do not know what will happen tomorrow.... You ought to say, 'If the Lord wills, we shall live and do this or that'" (James 4:14-15).

We don't know what tomorrow holds, but we know who holds tomorrow. Your Heavenly Father is already in your future, ready and able to make "all things work together" for your good (Romans 8:28).

Sleep on This:

The all-knowing, all-powerful God is already in your tomorrow. Nothing it brings will take Him by surprise. In the words of your Savior, "Therefore do not worry."

22

Preach
TO YOURSELF

And do not be conformed to this world, but be transformed by the renewing of your mind, that you may prove what is that good and acceptable and perfect will of God.

ROMANS 12:2

LISTEN

The late, great British pastor D. Martyn Lloyd-Jones once said, "Have you realized that most of your unhappiness in life is due to the fact that you are listening to yourself instead of talking to yourself?... You have to take yourself in hand, you have to address yourself, preach to yourself, question yourself. You must say to your soul: 'Why art thou cast down'—what business have you to be disquieted?... And then you must go on to remind yourself of God, Who God is, and what God is and what God has done, and what God has pledged Himself to do."[1]

It's true! Sometimes there's no one to give us a "talking to" but ourselves. We must remind ourselves of God's goodness. We must quote to ourselves the great promises of God. We must count our blessings and remember God's faithful mercies, doing this will renew our mind and relieve our worries.

Sleep on This:

As you lie down tonight, don't passively listen to the worries and fears of a restless mind. Talk to yourself proactively. Speak of God's faithful mercies and His great and precious promises.

23

Declare His

FAITHFULNESS TONIGHT

It is good to give thanks to the Lord, and to sing praises to Your name, O Most High; to declare Your lovingkindness in the morning, and Your faithfulness every night.

PSALM 92:1-2

LISTEN

One of the benefits of our Christian faith is the privilege of instant, direct access to heaven's throne. The line is always open. The Lord is always attentive. Romans 5:2 says that "we have gained access by faith into this grace in which we now stand" (NIV).

Of course, it's helpful to have a regular time and place for daily prayer. For many Christians that time is the morning. For other people the evening is best, or even their lunch break.

I would never presume to prescribe what is best for you. But I will encourage you to learn to end the day in prayer, thanking God as you fall asleep for some of the specific blessings you've encountered during the day. It's a powerful practice. As tonight's key Scripture verse reminds us, "It is good" to declare the Lord's faithfulness each night.

Sleep on This:

No matter how your day went, if you think back, there were some things today for which you can be grateful—mercies, kindnesses from your Heavenly Father. As you close your eyes in sleep, thank Him. Declare His faithfulness again and anew tonight.

24

A Lavish Love

WITHOUT BOUNDARIES

*And he arose and came to his father. But when he was still
a great way off, his father saw him and had compassion,
and ran and fell on his neck and kissed him.*

LUKE 15:20

LISTEN

God is frequently painted as someone who is angry, who sits in heaven with a big stick waiting to hit us, wanting to slap us down when we do wrong. But the one attribute about God I can never escape is His limitless love. He loves each of us as if we were the only one to love, and He loves us no matter what we have done.

This truth reminds me of the Prodigal Son. The word *prodigal* means "lavish, without restraint, no boundaries." Surely the father in this story was a prodigal, too, but in a different sense. He was lavish in his love. It was love with no boundaries, no restraints, no conditions—unconditional love from an unlimited source for an undeserving son.

Sleep on This:

Our Heavenly Father not only welcomes us back home, but He also comes searching for us when we're gone. He is a loving, searching, forgiving, restoring God.

— 25 —

Fear Not

*Fear not, for I am with you; be not dismayed, for I am
your God. I will strengthen you, yes, I will help you,
I will uphold you with My righteous right hand.*

ISAIAH 41:10

LISTEN

The "fear nots" of the Bible signify one of our greatest sources of comfort. If you're feeling worried, anxious, afraid, or insecure about something tonight, claim one of these verses:

- "Do not fear; for God has come to test you, and that His fear may be before you, so that you may not sin" (Exodus 20:20).

- "Be strong and of good courage, and do it; do not fear nor be dismayed, for the Lord God—my God—will be with you. He will not leave you nor forsake you" (1 Chronicles 28:20).

- "Do not fret—it only causes harm" (Psalm 37:8).

- "Do not fear, nor be afraid; have I not told you from that time, and declared it? You are My witnesses. Is there a God besides Me? Indeed there is no other Rock; I know not one" (Isaiah 44:8).

- "Do not fear therefore; you are of more value than many sparrows" (Matthew 10:31).

Sleep on This:

The God who spoke the universe into existence knows you. He loves you. And He is utterly faithful to keep His promises. You are secure in His hands. Ponder this truth and take comfort.

26

Worship

INSTEAD OF WORRYING

*Be still, be calm, see, and understand I am the True God. I am
honored among all the nations. I am honored over all the earth.*

PSALM 46:10, VOICE

LISTEN

When you're tempted to worry, worship instead. Instead of focusing on the conditions around you, focus on the kind Creator and Controller above you.

Music is an important factor in our worship. Only heaven knows how many times God's children have been delivered from their fears by singing the great hymns. This was one of Martin Luther's secrets. During some of his most discouraging and dangerous times, he studied Psalm 46, from which tonight's key verse is taken. Inspired by that psalm, Luther wrote his iconic hymn, "A Mighty Fortress." One stanza says:

> *And though this world, with devils filled,*
> *Should threaten to undo us,*
> *We will not fear, for God has willed*
> *His truth to triumph through us.*

In the quiet of this moment, turn your heart toward worship. Let it displace all worry.

Sleep on This:

The God to whom you belong is stronger than you can comprehend, more glorious than words can describe. He is a mighty fortress. And you are in that fortress because you are in Him.

27

True Security

For You, O Lord, will bless the righteous; with favor
You will surround him as with a shield.

PSALM 5:12

LISTEN

*W*e're living in a day in which everyone is increasingly security conscious. Here's great news. With Jesus we have one hundred percent security, and no one can ever breach the parameters of His love and care.

Indeed, as tonight's key verse declares, He surrounds us with His favor like a shield. Don't be too quick to disqualify yourself from that promise to "the righteous." None of us have any righteousness of our own. Yet 2 Corinthians 5:21 reveals that we believers have been made righteous with Jesus' own righteousness.

Remind yourself of God's promises. Search out your own "do not fear" passages in the Scripture. And rely on Him with one hundred percent of your faith for one hundred percent of your life throughout one hundred percent of your tomorrows. You'll find peace and rest within His shield of favor.

Sleep on This:

In this uncertain world, true security can only be found in one place—the mighty arms of your Heavenly Father. In Jesus you have been declared righteous. And with that declaration comes a level of security that those in the world can't know or comprehend.

—28—

He Is in Control

*The Lord is in control.... Yours is the mighty power and glory
and victory and majesty. Everything in the heavens and earth is
yours, O Lord .... We adore you as being in control of everything.*

1 KINGS 20:13, CEV; 1 CHRONICLES 29:11, TLB

LISTEN

*I*f someone were to ask you, "Is God sovereign?" You would likely answer, "Of course!" Most believers know that God is sovereign, yet sometimes the message doesn't get from our head to our heart.

As the two verses that comprise our key verses tonight make clear, the God who is in control is infinitely elevated above His creatures. He is the Most High. He is the Lord of heaven and earth. He is subject to none. He is influenced by none. He is absolutely independent, free, and in control. God does as He pleases, only as He pleases, always as He pleases, and forever as He pleases.

Don't fall prey to the lie that events and circumstances are beyond God's grasp.

Sleep on This:

You can take great comfort in knowing that the circumstances in our world and in your life haven't spiraled out of God's loving, redemptive control.

Guarded

BY INNUMERABLE SOLDIERS

Be anxious for nothing, but in everything by prayer and supplication, with thanksgiving, let your requests be made known to God; and the peace of God, which surpasses all understanding, will guard your hearts and minds through Christ Jesus.

PHILIPPIANS 4:6-7

LISTEN

The word "guard" in tonight's key verse is translated from a Greek military term meaning "to protect as with soldiers." Think of God's promises as a legion of soldiers sent to guard and protect your mind from anxious thoughts. These troops never tire. Never fall asleep while on guard duty. Never lose their nerve. Never flee in battle.

God's promises are untiring, unfailing, innumerable soldiers. Each is equipped for a special task, and there's a promise for every worry you harbor and for every need you face. God is faithful to keep all His promises. And that's why we can stand on the solid Rock in a fragile world.

Sleep on This:

Don't be anxious tonight—God's soldiers are on duty. With a heart of gratitude cast your cares and worries upon the Lord. And let the assurance of God's faithfulness guard your mind and flood your heart with peace.

— 30 —

A Big God

*Now to Him who is able to do exceedingly abundantly above all
that we ask or think, according to the power that works in us.*

EPHESIANS 3:20

LISTEN

*D*onald Grey Barnhouse is famous for classifying preachers as either "big god-ers" or "little god-ers." What he meant was that some seemed to preach a little God, while others proclaimed a big God—One who works miracles and is more than able to accomplish not only all His plans and purposes but also everything that concerns every single one of His people.

As tonight's key verse reminds us, we serve an incomprehensibly big God. This is an especially vital thing to keep in mind during the times in which we live. You have a God who desires to come into your life, whoever you may be and wherever you may be, and make a difference that only a big God can make.

Sleep on This:

Nothing is too hard for Him. Nothing takes Him by surprise. And He is exceedingly abundantly able to do big things in you and through you.

No Variation

IN GOD

Do not be deceived, my beloved brethren. Every good gift and every perfect gift is from above, and comes down from the Father of lights, with whom there is no variation or shadow of turning.

JAMES 1:16-17

LISTEN

*I*t's called "the change pandemic." Things in our world are changing so rapidly that the human mind (and heart) can't keep up. We're in a world that changes every single moment.

Enter God—unchanging, constant, immutable, eternal, and unalterably steadfast. How we need an unchangeable God at the core of our universe and in the center of our life!

If God were to change, that means He would either improve or regress. He cannot improve, for His perfections are infinite and eternal. He cannot regress, for He can never be less than He is. He is the same yesterday, today, and forever. He provides unshakable stability, like a mountain of granite in a desert of sand.

Sleep on This:

The world may be constantly changing, but you belong to a God who is immutable, unchanging, and steady. In Him "there is no variation or shadow of turning."

— 32 —

Always Present

*For this is what the high and exalted One says—he who lives
forever, whose name is holy: "I live in a high and holy place, but
also with the one who is contrite and lowly in spirit, to revive
the spirit of the lowly and to revive the heart of the contrite."*

ISAIAH 57:15, NIV

LISTEN

God is everywhere at the same time, yet God is not distant. It sounds like a contradiction because we think of life in terms of time and space. But God is not limited by time or space. He is the Creator of both.

Though He is present everywhere at the same time, there is no space that can contain Him. And while we're awed by the reality of God's universal presence in all quadrants of the universe, what we most need is the sense of His manifest presence here—His presence being near us to bless us.

Here's the wonderful news: We have a God who dwells with us and understands us and knows what it is like to be us.

Sleep on This:

It may be difficult to conceive, but God is not distant. He is present. Always. And especially so when you are struggling and "lowly in spirit."

—33—

Verses
THAT CALM

For the Lord your God is living among you. He is a mighty savior. He will take delight in you with gladness. With his love, he will calm all your fears. He will rejoice over you with joyful songs.

ZEPHANIAH 3:17, NLT

LISTEN

When the Israelites were trapped at the Red Sea, facing annihilation, Moses said to all the people, "Don't be afraid. Just stand still and watch the Lord rescue you today. The Egyptians you see today will never be seen again. The Lord himself will fight for you. Just stay calm" (Exodus 14:13-14, NLT).

In a crisis, before a single word of the Bible had been written, Moses spoke the word of the Lord to the Israelites. Today we have the Scriptures. And there is something powerful about exercising our assertive faith by claiming God's calming promises.

Allow God to speak to you through His Word. He will calm all your fears! He will do it with His love! He rejoices over you with joyful songs.

Sleep on This:

As tonight's key verse reminds us, no matter what circumstances you may be facing, you have a mighty, living Savior. And "with his love, he will calm all your fears."

— 34 —

Self-Calming

Surely I have calmed and quieted my soul, like a weaned child with his mother; like a weaned child is my soul within me.

PSALM 131:2

LISTEN

*E*xperts tell us that taking some very deep breaths can help us find some calm when we're anxious. That's good advice. God created our lungs, and when we fill them with His oxygen, it has a way of sending a small surge of relaxation through our bodies. Try it right now!

As you're taking that deep breath, open your heart for a fresh intake of His thoughts and for a reminder of who the Bible says you are. In tonight's key verse, we find David learning to calm himself. He might have seen in the distance a contented child being held in his mother's arms and thought, "That's how I feel in the arms of my Heavenly Father."

In a similar way, you can practice what David did—calming and quieting your soul by picturing the security you have in your Savior's everlasting arms.

Sleep on This:

As you lie down tonight, breathe deeply, and remind yourself that you are held safely and securely in the strong arms of a mighty, loving God.

— 35 —

Power for Living

But you will receive power when the Holy Spirit comes on you; and you will be my witnesses in Jerusalem, and in all Judea and Samaria, and to the ends of the earth.

ACTS 1:8, NIV

LISTEN

*T*rying to live the Christian life in your own strength in this sinful world is exhausting. We were never meant to live that way.

Many Christian people feel like they're on a treadmill, running as hard as they can but not making any progress. It can be difficult to stop long enough to realize that we're trying to do too much without the Source or power that God has given us. The Holy Spirit is our vital Source of power, not only to witness for Christ but also to do and be all that life requires.

Tonight, take a fresh look at this Person within you. He is within You to empower you and work through you.

Sleep on This:

You are not on your own. The Holy Spirit within you is an immense source of power. But He will not force Himself upon you. He simply stands by, ready to help when you come to the end of yourself.

Jehovah-Jireh

*Then Abraham lifted his eyes and looked, and there
behind him was a ram caught in a thicket by its horns.
So Abraham went and took the ram, and offered
it up for a burnt offering instead of his son.
And Abraham called the name of the place,
The-Lord-Will-Provide; as it is said to this day,
"In the Mount of the Lord it shall be provided."*

GENESIS 22:13-14

LISTEN

*I*n Hebrew, "The-Lord-Will-Provide" is Jehovah-Jireh. There's a deep lesson in this name, for Abraham's son Isaac was a symbol of Christ, the only begotten Son whom the Father offered as sacrifice for our sins on a mountain in Jerusalem, which is also known as Mount Moriah.

But there's also a lesson for us in our everyday life. We are deeply needy people, and sometimes we require emotional support, financial help, physical aid, or provisions related to an emergency or crisis. In such times we can approach Jehovah-Jireh on the throne of grace. We can call Him that, for He is the God who provides.

Sleep on This:

One of the sacred names of God is Jehovah-Jireh, "The-Lord-Will-Provide." Bring your needs before Him tonight.

— 37 —

Worthy of Praise

Praise be to the Lord, to God our Savior,
who daily bears our burdens.

PSALM 68:19, NIV

LISTEN

*O*ur Lord is our burden-bearer. If you've ever gone hiking with too much gear in your backpack, you know how quickly the weight can wear you down and how good it feels to slip that burden onto stronger shoulders! According to tonight's key verse, our God bears our burdens "daily."

The ESV translation renders that verse differently: "Blessed be the Lord, who daily bears us up." It's one thing if someone bears our burdens, but it's even better if they bear us up. When we find ourselves in troubled waters, the Lord and His Word are like rafts that buoy our souls. He lifts us up, carries us, and bears us along.

Finally, take a look at how the New King James Version handles that same verse: "Blessed be the Lord, Who daily loads us with benefits." Our Lord not only daily bears our burdens and bears us up, but He also daily loads us with blessings. Isn't that good news?

Sleep on This:

Our burden-bearing, uplifting, benefit-bestowing Heavenly Father is faithful and worthy of all our praise. Give your burdens to Him tonight.

Unthinkable,

BUT TRUE

For you did not receive the spirit of bondage again to fear, but you received the Spirit of adoption by whom we cry out, "Abba, Father." The Spirit Himself bears witness with our spirit that we are children of God.

ROMANS 8:15-16

LISTEN

"Abba": It is the most intimate Aramaic word for father. It actually means "Daddy." This is one of the most tender terms in the Bible.

No Jewish person in Jesus' day or earlier would have ever dreamed of using such an intimate term to address God. It was unthinkable. Yet Jesus always used it when referring to God. And He taught His disciples and us to do the same in prayer.

So when you are afraid, confused, or in pain, that's when you must cry out "Abba, Father." He hears you when you're at your lowest point. What could be more wonderful and glorious than to know that your Heavenly Father cares about you and that when you cry out to Him as "Abba, Father," He hears you?

Sleep on This:

You have been adopted by the God of the Universe. You are His child. He hears, and He cares. Cry out to your "Abba, Father" tonight.

— 39 —

Perfect Peace

You will keep him in perfect peace, whose mind
is stayed on You, because he trusts in You.

ISAIAH 26:3

LISTEN

*Y*ou can live with calmness and confidence because of the wonderful promise held in tonight's key verse. It's a conditional promise—that if we keep our mind stayed on God, He will keep us in perfect peace. Why? Because we trust in Him!

Yes, we're living in chaotic times but, to quote from Isaiah again, "In returning and rest you shall be saved; in quietness and confidence shall be your strength" (30:15). As we await the Lord's return, the posture of our heart should be calm, for Jesus said, "These things I have spoken to you, that in Me you may have peace" (John 16:33).

A heart that trusts in God can remain calm, compassionate, constructive, challenged, committed, and convinced—even in turbulent times.

Sleep on This:

Purpose to keep your heart stayed on God tonight. Trust in Him—in His goodness, His mercy, and His strength. Do so, and He will keep you in perfect peace.

— 40 —

Fear Insurance

*Yea, though I walk through the valley of the shadow
of death, I will fear no evil; for You are with me;
Your rod and Your staff, they comfort me.*

PSALM 23:4

LISTEN

*Y*ou likely have car insurance. But you might be a bit surprised to discover you can insure yourself against fear. The "policy" takes the form of promises from God's Word like the one that serves as tonight's key verse. But it's not the only one. Here are some others:

- "The Lord is my light and my salvation; whom shall I fear? The Lord is the strength of my life; of whom shall I be afraid?" (Psalm 27:1)

- "The Lord is on my side; I will not fear. What can man do to me?" (Psalm 118:6)

- "The fear of man brings a snare, but whoever trusts in the Lord shall be safe" (Proverbs 29:25).

Those verses, and others like them, are the best fear insurance you can find. Write them down, and place them in locations where you're prone to anxiety attacks. Hide them in your heart, and let the Word of God fortify your spirit.

Sleep on This:

Ponder these precious promises from God's Word as you lie down tonight. Hide them in your heart. And know that when fear-producing circumstances come your way, you'll be insured against letting fear take control.

— 41 —

Live Confidently

The Lord is my shepherd; I shall not want.
He makes me to lie down in green pastures;
He leads me beside the still waters.

PSALM 23:1-2

LISTEN

*N*othing is going to happen to you—ever—that will catch Jesus Christ by surprise. He is able to help His sheep work through anything, and not a single event will happen in the future that can change that.

That is why He commanded us to be of good cheer and not to let our heart be troubled, but instead to live with expectancy of what will happen on this earth (John 14:1; 16:33).

Live confidently in the light of Christ's imminent return. If you have put your faith in Him, even the tough times can be a magnet that draws you closer to the Good Shepherd.

Sleep on This:

Jesus is the Good Shepherd, and you are a beloved sheep of His flock. Be cheerful as you close your eyes tonight. Your Shepherd keeps watch. And nothing tomorrow brings will catch Him by surprise.

A Love

BEYOND REASON

For he chose us in him before the creation of the world to be holy and blameless in his sight. In love he predestined us for adoption to sonship through Jesus Christ, in accordance with his pleasure and will.

EPHESIANS 1:4-5, NIV

LISTEN

*G*od loves you. Why? Simply because He decided to do so. That's the amazing message of tonight's key verse. Adopting you was "in accordance with his pleasure and will." Of course, He loves everyone, no matter who we are, where we come from, or what we've done. In a sense, God's love is unreasonable.

If you look at it from the human perspective, there are abundant reasons for God *not* to love us. Yet God just pushes past all of that, and He loves us simply because it's His nature to love.

Paul tells us in the Bible that we are unreasonably loved by God. For instance, in Romans 5:8 we read, "But God demonstrates His own love toward us, in that while we were still sinners, Christ died for us."

Sleep on This:

Don't try to understand it. Simply accept it. You are loved by God just as you are. And He loves you too much to leave you as you are.

— 43 —

He Hears.

HE CARES.

Now this is the confidence that we have in Him, that if
we ask anything according to His will, He hears us.
And if we know that He hears us, whatever we ask, we know
that we have the petitions that we have asked of Him.

1 JOHN 5:14-15

LISTEN

One of our greatest benefits as believers is the privilege and power of prayer. On the cross Jesus opened the way for us to approach the throne of grace with boldness.

My friend Rob Morgan wrote, "Prayer is the lever that can exert a force much greater than its size. It's a fulcrum that tilts our circumstances grace-ward. It's a wedge that allows us to open doors and to exert influence. It's a pulley that lifts us upward while simultaneously drawing down the provisions of heaven. It's the axle on which the abundant life turns. What a tool is prayer!"[2]

He is right. The Lord's answers aren't always instant and dramatic, but they are always wisely bestowed. Finish this day with a simple, heartfelt prayer to your Heavenly Father. He hears.

Sleep on This:

You belong to a God who hears. Jesus' extraordinary sacrifice opened the way to His presence. His throne is a throne of grace.

— 44 —

Time to Simplify?

*God anointed Jesus of Nazareth with the Holy Spirit
and with power, who went about doing good.*

ACTS 10:38

LISTEN

*S*wamped? Overwhelmed? Remember: The Lord doesn't expect you to do everything. The key is to follow His example and simply—keep the main thing the main thing.

His whole life was characterized by simplicity because He didn't feel the need to have everything or do everything. In tonight's key verse, we find Peter describing Jesus as not only being God's Anointed, but also as Someone who "went about doing good."

Notice that Jesus didn't go around doing *everything*. He went around doing good. When Jesus ascended to heaven after three years of ministry, Israel was still filled with those who were sick, blind, lame, and lost.

But He did what He came to do. He focused on the Father's will.

Sleep on This:

Think of ways you can simplify your life. Ask your Heavenly Father to show you areas in which you're carrying burdens or owning tasks He hasn't called you to carry or own.

45

Three Ps

TO COMBAT WORRY

*Therefore do not worry, saying, "What shall we eat?"
or "What shall we drink?" or "What shall we wear?"
For after all these things the Gentiles seek. For your
heavenly Father knows that you need all these things.*

MATTHEW 6:31-32

LISTEN

*W*orry is a particularly virulent form of fear. Someone once said that worry is a trickle of fear that meanders through the mind until it cuts a channel into which all other thoughts drain.

We all worry. But ideally, it's a momentary phase, not a lifestyle. For many people, worry has become so ingrained in their personalities that once the old worries are gone, they search for new ones.

That's why fear and worry are sins—they doubt God's promises, question His power, disregard His presence, and divert our heart from His praise. John Wesley said, "I would no more worry than I would curse or swear." How, then, do we defeat fear and worry? With three God-given weapons of our own: prayer, promises, and perseverance!

Sleep on This:

Worry has no place in our heart. So tonight, replace it with the three powerful weapons at your disposal. Pray about your concerns. Put yourself in remembrance of God's promises. And purpose to persevere in your faith!

46

God Keeps Watch

In the world you will have tribulation;
but be of good cheer, I have overcome the world.

JOHN 16:33

LISTEN

A 24-hour news cycle, ubiquitous social media hysteria, and a bad-news ticker in the palm of every person's hand (disguised as a phone)—have all combined to bring us a constant stream of alarming headlines.

In the face of this, how wonderful to know that through the sunshine and shadows of time and history, God keeps watch over His own. That's why we shouldn't let the headlines trouble us. Because behind them are the strong, caring hands and watchful eyes of our Heavenly Father.

We shouldn't let the news reports disturb our peace, for His mercies are new every morning. We shouldn't let breaking news vanquish our peace of mind; we should instead break out in song that "Our God Reigns." The Bible says we will "have no fear of bad news" if our heart is steadfast, trusting in Him (Psalm 112:7, NIV).

Sleep on This:

No matter what the news of the day brings, have no fear. You can be of good cheer because the Savior you serve and who loves you has overcome the world.

47

No Need

TO WORRY ABOUT MONEY

He who did not spare His own Son,
but delivered Him up for us all, how shall He
not with Him also freely give us all things?

ROMANS 8:32

LISTEN

*I*f there was ever a time Christians needed to depend on the Lord's provision, it's now. If you're anxious about making ends meet, consider the wonderful promise of tonight's key verse. It's one of scores of biblical promises that assure us that we don't need to worry about provision or material things.

For example, the psalmist declared, "I have been young, and now am old; yet I have not seen the righteous forsaken, nor his descendants begging bread" (Psalm 37:25). And remember Psalm 34:9-10 which says, "Oh, fear the Lord, you His saints! There is no want to those who fear Him. The young lions lack and suffer hunger; but those who seek the Lord shall not lack any good thing."

Sleep on This:

You have a God who has promised to meet your needs. And you not only have the Scriptures but also four thousand years' worth of testimonies from biblical and Church history that assure you of God's provision.

48

Faith

IN HIS FAITHFULNESS

*And my God shall supply all your need according
to His riches in glory by Christ Jesus.*

PHILIPPIANS 4:19

LISTEN

*I*f you're anxious about how your needs are going to be met, here are a few time-tested biblical suggestions. First, tell God about your needs, humbly and honestly. Make it a matter of earnest prayer.

Secondly, read through a list of biblical promises like the one that serves as tonight's key verse. With pen in hand, circle the verse or verses that most encourage you. Look up any passage you've circled and read it in its fuller context. Then memorize and claim it for yourself as an act of faith.

Finally, remember our Lord's lesson in Matthew 6 about God's care for the birds (verses 25-27). Remind yourself that you are worth far more than many sparrows.

Sleep on This:

God is faithful. He is kind. And you can count on Him to meet your needs as you keep your eyes on Him. Rest in His promises.

— 49 —

The God
OF EVERY DAY

*And He said to me, "My grace is sufficient for you,
for My strength is made perfect in weakness."
Therefore most gladly I will rather boast in my infirmities,
that the power of Christ may rest upon me.*

2 CORINTHIANS 12:9

LISTEN

God is not only the God of heaven and earth; He's the God of every day. He's a God who never faces an impossible task. He brings order from disorder, efficiency from confusion, and hope from despair. There's no need to feel overwhelmed when you are a child of God.

You can trust God to turn your impossibilities into accomplishments as you turn your days and your duties over to Him. God specializes in handling the day-to-day issues in your life, and your breaking points are often the starting points for His grace. Take charge of your life by letting Him take charge of you.

Sleep on This:

There is no detail of your daily life that God does not care about, no concern in your heart that does not matter to Him. So breathe and rest. The God of heaven and earth considers you His own.

50

Let the Lord

BE YOUR CONFIDENCE

Do not be afraid of sudden terror, nor of trouble from the wicked when it comes; for the Lord will be your confidence.

PROVERBS 3:25-26

LISTEN

*Y*ears ago, advice columnist Ann Landers was asked if there was a common denominator among the thousands of letters that came to her each week. She said the great overriding theme of all the letters was fear.

It seems the two most dangerous saboteurs are found within our own heart—the diabolical duo of fear and worry. They stalk us whenever we board an airplane, open a bill, visit a doctor, walk down a darkened sidewalk, or glance at the clock when a child is late for curfew.

That should not be so for the child of God. Indeed, tonight's key verse brings us a command. We are told *not* to be afraid of some sudden, terrifying event or of "trouble from the wicked when it comes."

Sleep on This:

Although we are almost certainly living in the Last Days, that doesn't mean we have a license to live in dread and anxiety. On the contrary, we are commanded by the Word of God not to be afraid. As you lay your head down tonight, let the Lord be your confidence.

51

The "Peace"

OF THE PUZZLE

Peace I leave with you, My peace I give to you; not as the world gives do I give to you. Let not your heart be troubled, neither let it be afraid.

JOHN 14:27

LISTEN

*W*hat in the world is going on? While that is a question we often have to wait until the end of the day to answer, there is a question we can answer first thing every morning in our Bibles: *Who* in the world is going on? And the answer is always and ever, "Our God."

Although we live in puzzling times, life does not have to be a puzzle to the person who knows God. The Savior, who told His original disciples, "My peace I give to you.... Let not your heart be troubled, neither let it be afraid," says the same thing to us today.

There is nothing happening in our world that the Word of God has not already addressed. There is nothing that God has not foreseen. Your Bible holds all the pieces to tomorrow's puzzle. And if you know Jesus Christ personally, you possess the "peace" of the puzzle as well.

Sleep on This:

Do not lay down with a troubled heart tonight. Don't let your heart be afraid. Jesus has left His peace with you. Life may be a puzzle. But He is the "peace" of the puzzle.

— 52 —

The Unfailing
COMPASSION OF GOD

*For all the promises of God in Him are Yes, and in
Him Amen, to the glory of God through us.*

2 CORINTHIANS 1:20

LISTEN

*I*n Lamentations 3:23 Jeremiah says of God, "Great is Your faithfulness." The Hebrew word Jeremiah used for "faithfulness" is the term *aman*, which means "so be it." It's the word from which we get our English word *amen*.

God is the "amen" of every one of His promises. As tonight's key verse reminds us, "For all the promises of God in Him are Yes, and in Him Amen" (2 Corinthians 1:20).

God's faithfulness stands in the very center of His creation, but it also resides in the core of His revelation because faithfulness means keeping one's word. God's faithfulness allows us to have total confidence in every promise He has written down for us in His Word, and that frees us from the grip of anxious worry.

Sleep on This:

Your compassionate God has already provided an amen to every one of His promises. You can have total confidence in every one of them. Oh, how great is His faithfulness!

No Expiration Date

Forever, O Lord, Your word is settled in heaven.
Your faithfulness endures to all generations;
You established the earth, and it abides.

PSALM 119:89-90

LISTEN

*Y*our refrigerator and kitchen pantry are both filled with items that have an expiration date. They have a shelf life, after which they can no longer be counted on to be safe or nutritious.

The promises of God, however, have no expiration date. Their shelf life is eternity. They are as enduring as His inspired Word and as trustworthy as His unchanging nature. His promises, which cover every moment of our life, are as certain as His character.

Jesus is "the faithful witness, the firstborn from the dead, and the ruler over the kings of the earth" (Revelation 1:5). His resurrection is the sign and seal of God's power to guarantee His Word to us forever. The Bible ends with the ringing declaration: "These words are faithful and true" (Revelation 22:6). Because of His unending, inexhaustible faithfulness, God's promises are as fresh and dependable as the day He spoke them.

Sleep on This:

Tonight, take great comfort in the knowledge that God's promises have no expiration date. His faithfulness endures to all generations, including yours.

— 54 —

He Hears.

HE ANSWERS.

*Call to Me, and I will answer you, and show you great
and mighty things, which you do not know.*

JEREMIAH 33:3

LISTEN

*W*hat a privilege it is—God's open invitation to come to Him in prayer. It is mind-boggling if you stop to think about it. He hears. He listens. What is even more astonishing is that we can pray with expectancy!

Because God is faithful, we can have confidence when we pray. Through Christ, we can be in touch with God instantly. Psalm 143:1 says, "Lord, hear my prayer, listen to my cry for mercy; in your faithfulness and righteousness come to my relief" (NIV).

How can we be confident God hears our prayers? Because it is the nature of God to be faithful, to be constant and consistent in who He is, and to come to our relief. As tonight's key verse reveals, "Call to me," God says. "I will answer you," He promises. God's faithfulness assures you of answered prayer.

Sleep on This:

As you turn out the lights and settle into bed, God is there, waiting to hear from you. His faithfulness keeps the door open, and His heart is consistently, constantly inclined toward you. Bring your prayers to Him.

—55—

Protected

*But the Lord is faithful, who will establish
you and guard you from the evil one.*

2 THESSALONIANS 3:3

LISTEN

*W*e know there is spiritual danger all around us. Yet God is faithful in keeping us from evil and from the evil one. That's why Jesus told us to request protection from the Father against him. In His model prayer in Matthew 6:13, Jesus says, "And do not lead us into temptation, but deliver us from the evil one."

In His High Priestly Prayer in John 17, Jesus petitioned the Father, saying, "I do not pray that You should take them out of the world, but that You should keep them from the evil one" (verse 15).

Tonight you can pray, "Lord, I have no idea what's going to be in my path tomorrow, but with confidence I can ask, 'Lead me not into temptation, but deliver me from the evil one.'" Do so, and the faithfulness of God will answer back: "Because I am faithful, I will establish you and guard you from the evil one."

Sleep on This:

The God of infinite power and might watches over you. Jesus Himself prayed that the Father would keep you from the power of the evil one. And He is faithful to deliver you.

56

Unconditional

FAITHFULNESS

If we are faithless, He remains faithful;
He cannot deny Himself.

2 TIMOTHY 2:13

LISTEN

When we come face-to-face with God's faithfulness, our natural impulse is to contrast that with our own faithlessness and mistakes. But even in this, we find strength in tonight's key Scripture. Even when we are faithless, He remains faithful.

If you're a Jesus follower but feel defeated by your failures, you are not alone. Be encouraged that God's faithfulness to you is not conditional on your faithfulness to Him. He is faithful to you no matter what. His faithfulness extends right into our failures. The Bible says, "If we confess our sins, *He is faithful* and just to forgive us our sins and to cleanse us from all unrighteousness" (1 John 1:9, emphasis added).

Sleep on This:

The faithfulness of God touches your life in countless ways. Because God is faithful even when you are faithless, you can rest in His promises, you can pray with confidence, you can overcome evil in your life, and you can be forgiven.

57

You Are Loved

AS YOU ARE

But God, who is rich in mercy, because of His great love with which He loved us, even when we were dead in trespasses, made us alive together with Christ (by grace you have been saved).

EPHESIANS 2:4-5

LISTEN

*I*t's hard for us to find someone willing to love us as we are. But God does, and He does it perfectly. The Bible says, "God is love." It doesn't merely say He is loving. He is that without a doubt. But the Bible says He is love—that God is the very embodiment of love, the personification of love, and the essence of all that love means (1 John 4:8, 16).

As we look at this aspect of God's nature, we discover a Creator who loves us as we are. He never asks us to get rid of our baggage before He accepts us. He takes us as we are.

Sleep on This:

You are being transformed by grace. But from the beginning and continually throughout eternity, you have a God who looks at you just as you are and says, "I love you."

58

Your Times

ARE IN HIS HAND

*To everything there is a season, a time for
every purpose under heaven.*

ECCLESIASTES 3:1

LISTEN

*G*od controls the times and the seasons, and history unfolds according to His preordained purposes. When Jesus died on the cross, it was by "the determined purpose and foreknowledge of God" (Acts 2:23). And He controls the chronology of the lives of His people too. The Bible says, "It is appointed for men to die once" (Hebrews 9:27). God knows the day of your birth. And He knows the day of your death long before it will happen.

He is in control of the times and the seasons of your life. The Bible says, "My times are in Your hand" (Psalm 31:15). One of the most beautiful passages in the Bible about this subject begins with tonight's key verse. There is a time for everything in your life. And your loving Heavenly Father's purposes for you are good.

Sleep on This:

You don't know what tomorrow holds, but your Heavenly Father does. Trust Him with your times and seasons. They are in His loving hand.

— 59 —

He Finishes

WHAT HE STARTS

*He who has begun a good work in you will
complete it until the day of Jesus Christ.*

PHILIPPIANS 1:6

LISTEN

*C*hange is at the heart of our growth as Christians. The apostle Paul said, "But we all, with unveiled face, beholding as in a mirror the glory of the Lord, are being transformed into the same image from glory to glory, just as by the Spirit of the Lord" (2 Corinthians 3:18).

As we live in Christ's presence, worship Him, behold Him, and study the Scripture, the Holy Spirit unleashes a process of change within us. We are constantly being transformed from one degree of glory (or Christlikeness) to another. We are being conformed into the image of His Son.

Change is at the heart of redemption. Every phase of justification, sanctification, and glorification involves progress and transformation until one day in heaven we'll be eternally like Christ. That's very encouraging because, if you're like me, you can recognize things in your life that need to change. Thank God we have the precious promise of tonight's key verse.

Sleep on This:

God has begun a good work in you. Be assured that He will complete it.

— 60 —

Not One Word

*And you know in all your hearts and in all your souls
that not one thing has failed of all the good things which
the Lord your God spoke concerning you. All have come
to pass for you; not one word of them has failed.*

JOSHUA 23:14

LISTEN

*T*he Bible is packed with so many promises it's hard to count them. One man tried. A Canadian schoolteacher named Everek Storms had already read through the Bible 26 times. So in conjunction with his twenty-seventh reading, over the span of a year and a half, he read and counted all the promises.[3]

He came up with more than 7,000 promises made by Almighty God to humans—7,487 to be exact. That's more than 20 promises a day over the course of a full year!

It is one thing to have a huge reservoir of promises. It's another to know that they are unfailingly true. You see, these promises can never waver because the God who made them cannot change. He doesn't change His mind, and His grace doesn't come and go, vacillate, seesaw, or expire.

Sleep on This:

Not one word of God's promises has ever failed. Or ever will. Ponder that as you close your eyes tonight.

Turn Fear

INTO F.E.A.R.

Have I not commanded you? Be strong and of good courage; do not be afraid, nor be dismayed, for the Lord your God is with you wherever you go.

JOSHUA 1:9

LISTEN

*W*henever I'm anxious or afraid, I've learned a way to turn fear inside out. I discovered I can turn fear into the acronym, F.E.A.R., mapping out four key steps.

F: Faith. When fear comes knocking at our heart's door, let faith answer. Faith is God's antidote for fear. When we can't control the results, we can extol the Redeemer. When our hands are tied, our knees will still bend in trust. Taking this step leads to...

E: Expectancy. It sends a positive force into our heart to strengthen us. We expect our Lord to work, to move, to do what only He can do. Then we can remember that God is...

A: Almighty. We do not have a weak God. Our God cannot grow weary; He cannot misunderstand or mislead. He cannot fail. When we take these three steps, it enables us to...

R: Rest. We can rest in His promises. Rest in His sovereignty. Rest in His love. Rest in His grace. And rest in His ability to deliver us from all our fears.

Sleep on This:

Tonight, as you close your eyes, run through these four steps in your heart and mind. Choose faith and expectancy. Remind yourself that your Heavenly Father is Almighty. Now breathe deeply and... rest.

—62—

The Same God

When the water in the skin was gone, [Hagar] put the boy under one of the bushes.... Then God opened her eyes and she saw a well of water. So she went and filled the skin with water and gave the boy a drink.

GENESIS 21:15, 19, NIV

LISTEN

The same God who provided a spring of water for Hagar, created streams in the desert for the Israelites, brought bread by ravens for Elijah, delivered fish for a multitude on the Galilean hillside and food for the widows in the book of Acts will also provide for you.

He is the Father of lights—the Maker of the stars—and He knows how to meet the needs of His children.

Because the Lord is our Shepherd, we have everything we need (Psalm 23:1). If we seek first His Kingdom and His righteousness, "all these things" will be given to us as well (Matthew 6:33). Our God will supply all our need out of "His riches in glory by Christ Jesus" (Philippians 4:19).

Sleep on This:

The same God who provided for the heroes of the Bible cares for you, and His giving heart remains the same.

Your Well-Being

MATTERS

Then the Lord said to him, "Peace be with you; do not fear, you shall not die." So Gideon built an altar there to the Lord, and called it The-Lord-Is-Peace. To this day it is still in Ophrah of the Abiezrites.

JUDGES 6:23-24

LISTEN

Tonight's key verse presents another of the sacred Hebrew names of God found in the Old Testament. The Hebrew phrase translated "The-Lord-Is-Peace" here is Jehovah-Shalom.

Do you know the wonderful Hebrew word, *shalom*? It means "peace" and also connotes wholeness, soundness, and well-being. We can use that name in prayer whenever we're afraid. Jehovah-Shalom: He is our peace!

No wonder the Bible exhorts us in Philippians 4:6-7 to "not be anxious about anything, but in every situation, by prayer and petition, with thanksgiving, present your requests to God." When we do, we're promised that "the peace of God, which transcends all understanding, will guard your hearts and your minds in Christ Jesus" (NIV).

Sleep on This:

Any time you're afraid or anxious, you can call on the Heavenly Father who is also called, "The-Lord-Is-Peace." Your well-being matters to Him!

— 64 —

God, Our Sustainer

He is before all things, and in him all things hold together.

COLOSSIANS 1:17, ESV

LISTEN

What would happen if, for a single moment, Almighty God withdrew His hand from the universe? It would fly off into oblivion and chaos. It would collapse like a building imploding. As tonight's key verse reveals, He is the One who holds the universe together. He is the God who preserves the world in which we live. He is power.

And, of course, since He sustains His universe, how much more does He sustain His own people who are in the universe? That includes you. He knows how to care for you and keep you.

Psalm 55:22 says, "Cast your burden on the Lord, and He shall sustain you; He shall never permit the righteous to be moved." During a very difficult time in his life, David wrote, "I lay down and slept; I awoke, for the Lord sustained me" (Psalm 3:5).

Sleep on This:

Take a cue from David. Lay down and sleep tonight in the comforting knowledge that the God you serve is your Sustainer. He is always and ever with you.

He Dresses

IN FAITHFULNESS

Let us hold fast the confession of our hope without wavering, for He who promised is faithful.

HEBREWS 10:23

LISTEN

When you stop and think about why so many people are unfaithful these days, you can compile a long list. Some people are simply too lazy to do what they've promised. Their resolve gives out, and they don't have stamina for the long haul. Sometimes their unfaithfulness is the result of desire, fear, weakness, loss of interest, or outside influence. But none of these things can affect God. He is not lazy, and His resolve never slackens.

You serve a God who can be trusted. He never forgets, never falters, and never fails. He always keeps His Word, and there is no possibility of Him ever changing. Faithfulness is the very clothing God wears, for Isaiah 11:5 says, "Righteousness shall be the belt of His loins, and faithfulness the belt of His waist."

Sleep on This:

You can trust your Heavenly Father. Always. He wears faithfulness like a garment. Whatever concerns you tonight, you can confidently leave it in His hands.

— 66 —

Rest for Your Soul

Come to Me, all you who labor and are heavy laden, and I will give you rest. Take My yoke upon you and learn from Me, for I am gentle and lowly in heart, and you will find rest for your souls. For My yoke is easy and My burden is light.

MATTHEW 11:28-30

LISTEN

The invitation in tonight's key Scripture is not recorded in any of the other Gospels. Jesus looked around and saw people staggering under burdens of oppression and the demands of lifeless religious obligation. Jesus stood up in the midst of those Jewish people with arms outstretched and said, "Come to Me... and I will give you rest."

What He said to that generation is the same invitation that He offers to us in our generation today. Jesus, in His invitation, speaks to all who are burdened by overwork and responsibility and anxiety and stress and tension.

He says, "Come now to Me all of you who experience this, and I will give you rest."

Sleep on This:

Even as you lie down to rest tonight, Jesus still says, "Come to Me." With Him you will find rest for your soul.

God's Overflowing
GOODNESS

*The Lord is good to all, and His tender
mercies are over all His works.*

PSALM 145:9

LISTEN

"God is good." It's an oft-spoken cliché. But it's far more than that. It is a fundamental biblical truth. Declaring God's goodness speaks to His excellence and His attitude of benevolent grace toward all. It means He is gracious. He is merciful. When we say, "God is good," we're talking about His perfection and His excellence.

The more you study the word *good* in the Bible, the more one central concept will jump out at you. God's goodness conveys His infinitely generous attitude toward us. By nature, He longs to bring blessing and joy to all His creatures.

Exodus 34:6 declares, "The Lord, the Lord God, merciful and gracious, longsuffering, and abounding in goodness and truth."

That is the heart of our Father in heaven. It is His delight to do good for all who are His. God's goodness is His very nature. He is abundantly good; His goodness overflows.

Sleep on This:

The God who loves you, chose you, and made you His own is good—abundantly, overflowingly good.

— 68 —

Not Forgotten

Though I walk in the midst of trouble, You will
revive me... and Your right hand will save me.
The Lord will perfect that which concerns me; Your mercy,
O Lord, endures forever; do not forsake the works of Your hands.

PSALM 138:7-8

LISTEN

*D*avid knew something vitally important. In times of trouble, we need to give voice to our confidence in God. In tonight's key verse, David describes walking "in the midst of trouble." It's one thing to have a need or two. It's another to be so surrounded by trouble that your days feel like a hike through a forest of problems.

Nevertheless, David declared confidence in God's power, His "right hand." What's more, not only will the Lord protect you, He will "perfect" you.

The Lord will perfect, that is complete, the things that concern you. God is working on you and in you. And His purpose is to perfect and complete you, making you mature and whole.

Sleep on This:

God has not forgotten you. The plan you thought He had for your life has not been abandoned. Your faithful Father will perfect and complete that which concerns you.

69

Provision

IN DUE SEASON

The eyes of all look expectantly to You, and You give them their food in due season. You open Your hand and satisfy the desire of every living thing.

PSALM 145:15-16

LISTEN

$\mathcal{M}$ ost of us struggle with various fears, and many of those anxieties represent a lack of faith in God's abundant goodness for us. The psalmist said, "I would have lost heart, unless I had believed that I would see the goodness of the Lord in the land of the living" (Psalm 27:13).

We could spare ourselves a lot of anguish by simply meditating more on God's kindness and goodness. It's remarkable to think about, but when we're in the will of God through Christ, we will never face a genuine need for which God doesn't give genuine provision.

He who gave us lungs created air. He who gave us stomachs supplies food and water. He who made us in His image provided companionship. He who made us with eyes also created spellbinding vistas so that we can enjoy their beauty. He who made us with eternal souls also provided a pathway to heaven through our Lord Jesus.

Sleep on This:

God, in due season, will happily and graciously provide for every one of your needs.

70

He Knows,

AND HE LOVES YOU ANYWAY

Before a word is on my tongue you, Lord, know it completely.

PSALM 139:4, NIV

LISTEN

*Y*ou can rejoice in God's omniscience, that is, His absolute and complete knowledge of everything. You can enjoy the security of knowing He knows you—knows all about you—yet loves you still.

His love and His omniscience are both infinite, which means He can never know us better or love us less. Psalm 1:6 says, "The Lord knows the way of the righteous." And Job testified, "He knows the way that I take" (Job 23:10).

Because of the finished work of Jesus on the cross, you can access God. There aren't any hidden skeletons in your closet that will deflect His love from you. No talebearer can ever give God new information about you because He already knows everything. No enemy can make a false accusation stick against you because God already knows the truth. There is no unsuspected weakness in your character that can change His attitude toward you.

God knows you with endless knowledge, and He loves you with everlasting love.

Sleep on This:

With God—and with God alone—you can be fully transparent and totally intimate.

71

He Rules

AND REIGNS

Whatever the Lord pleases He does, in heaven and in earth, in the seas and in all deep places.

PSALM 135:6

LISTEN

God is in charge. He is on His throne and always will be. He rules and reigns in the affairs of men worldwide, from history to prophecy, from sea to sea, from time to eternity.

The child of God can take great comfort in the knowledge that God is infinitely mighty. You can rest in the knowledge that the One who loves you and made you His own is sovereign.

When we say God is sovereign, we mean He is in charge of everything. The phrase "God is in control" is no trite cliché. It is a proclamation of eternal truth.

There is no place in heaven or earth where God's plans and purposes are being thwarted. That means nothing you face today took God by surprise. In fact, He is already at work in your tomorrow.

Sleep on This:

The world is not spinning out of control. Your circumstances haven't slipped from God's grasp. He is ruling and reigning.

72

In Trouble

HE IS NEAR

God is our refuge and strength, a very present help in trouble.

PSALM 46:1

LISTEN

When going through deep waters, difficult times, and hard experiences, it is vital to meditate on our ever-present God. We can find great strength in recalling the Lord's promise, "I am with you." The Bible tells us God's presence is always available, but it is manifest at certain times, and those include times of trouble.

Notice each of these words in tonight's key verse: *A very present help in trouble.*

Is God more present with you in trouble than at any other time? No. But His manifest presence is there to help you, comfort you, guide you, and direct you.

Nothing comforts us more in our troubles than meditating on the verses in God's Word that assure us of His nearness and presence. Psalm 73:28 says, "But as for me, it is good to be near God" (NIV).

Sleep on This:

In difficult times... in deep waters... God says, "I am your refuge. I am your strength. I am very present and ready to help."

— 73 —

Remember His
MARVELOUS WORKS

Remember His marvelous works which He has done,
His wonders, and the judgments of His mouth.

PSALM 105:5

LISTEN

On a page, a sentence in Hebrew reads from right to left. Most of us are used to reading from left to right, so for us reading Hebrew would be a backward experience.

God's providence and God's faithfulness are like reading Hebrew. And that's also the way we need to read the story of our life. God's faithfulness runs for all eternity. Only by looking back over our life can we see the way He has led us. But whether we look backward, forward, or simply around us—He is faithful.

Life is full of challenges and problems. But God is faithful, and that trumps all our tears and tragedies. When the psalmist reminded himself of that, he rejoiced and gave thanks to the Lord.

Sleep on This:

Think back across the years of your life. Remember all the times God's faithfulness and goodness saw you through hardships. Consider His marvelous works and praise Him.

74

Infinite Patience

For the Lord is good; His mercy is everlasting,
and His truth endures to all generations.

PSALM 100:5

LISTEN

*I*n a sense, all the blessings of God can be organized into two categories: grace and mercy. Grace is God giving us what we do not deserve. Mercy is God withholding from us what we do deserve.

The word "mercy" in tonight's key verse speaks directly to God's amazing, infinite patience. The mercy of God equals the patience of God, which is endless, infinite, and an outgrowth of His goodness.

Psalm 107 speaks beautifully of what God has done for us in His merciful, patient goodness. Verses 10 through 12 speak of the terrible predicaments we get ourselves into—the storms of life. But there is wonderful news in verse 13: "Then they cried out to the Lord in their trouble, and He saved them out of their distresses."

Sleep on This:

Your Heavenly Father is patient. He hears you in your distress and patiently brings you out of trouble. His mercy is inexhaustible.

75

Your Wits

ARE NEVER ENOUGH

They... are at their wits' end. Then they cry out to the Lord in their trouble, and He brings them out of their distresses. He calms the storm, so that its waves are still.

PSALM 107:27-29

LISTEN

*H*ave you ever been at your "wits' end"? The people described in tonight's key verse from Psalms were sailors out at sea, caught in a ferocious storm.

It can often feel as if you and I are those sailors, staggering around on the deck of a heaving, storm-tossed ship, holding on for dear life. Like those sailors in the psalm, our best and only recourse is to cry out to God.

In Mark 4:39, when Jesus rebuked the waves and wind during a storm on the sea, the Bible says: "The wind ceased and there was a great calm." He calmed the storm that day, and He can calm the storm in your life. He still calms storms.

Sleep on This:

You may feel that you're at your "wits' end." That is actually a good place to be because our wits are never enough. We sometimes need to come to the end of ourselves. Then we can rest in the assurance that "He calms the storm, so that its waves are still."

76

The Power

OF REMEMBERING

I will remember the works of the Lord; surely
I will remember Your wonders of old.

PSALM 77:11

LISTEN

When we recall how our Heavenly Father has kept His promises in the past, it enables us to trust Him for future endeavors. We not only rest on His promises, but we also act on them by tackling His work with enthusiasm. Like the beloved hymn says, we have "strength for today and bright hope for tomorrow" because of His great faithfulness.

The Lord has something for you to do—something for which He has been preparing you. The next step is always built on prior experiences, and we shouldn't be afraid of the future.

Never has a word from Almighty God failed, and never has Jesus not done as He has said. He is faithful and true. We should understand, underline, undergird, and undertake as we appreciate His faithfulness and appropriate the promises that stand out on every page of His Word.

Sleep on This:

God is the same yesterday, today, and forever. He keeps His promises. As you close your eyes, remember the times He has demonstrated His faithfulness to you. As He has been faithful in your past, so He will be faithful in your future.

77

Deep Rest

There remains therefore a rest for the people of God.
For he who has entered His rest has himself also
ceased from his works as God did from His.

HEBREWS 4:9-10

LISTEN

*I*f you're familiar with the Genesis creation account, you know that God spent six days in creative activity and then rested on the seventh day. Later, for their good and blessing, God echoed this by instituting a weekly Sabbath for Israel. Every seventh day, they were to rest.

Do you know what the Jewish people did with it? Just what we would have done. They turned a blessing into a burden. They took what was supposed to be a time of refreshment and made it the scariest, most complicated day of the week.

How often do we do the same thing? Tonight's key verses reveal that the Christian life should be a type of ongoing Sabbath rest. The author is not talking about passivity and lethargy. He's talking about a quality of life. It's the kind of life that the Lord wants us to have.

Sleep on This:

Have you turned blessings into burdens? It's time to enter into the deep rest that only comes from following God with a heart of trust.

78

Undivide

YOUR MIND

And Jesus answered and said to her, "Martha, Martha, you are worried and troubled about many things. But one thing is needed, and Mary has chosen that good part, which will not be taken away from her."

LUKE 10:41-42

LISTEN

*Y*ou no doubt are familiar with the context of tonight's key verse—the contrast between Mary and Martha when Jesus visited their home. While He was there, Jesus noticed that Martha was overcome with worries.

In the New Testament, the Greek word for "worry," *merimnao*, is a compound word formed from two words. One means "to divide," and the other means "the mind." So from a biblical standpoint, worry is a divided mind.

In this sense, a worried mind is one with two conflicting agendas. One agenda is for things which are life-giving and good. The other is for things which are destructive and move you away from what is most important. No wonder James wrote in his epistle that a double-minded man is unstable in all of his ways (James 1:8).

Sleep on This:

Tonight, you can choose "the good part." Focus on your Savior, His will, and His ways. Undivide your mind. Release your worries to Him.

79

Ponder

HIS FAITHFULNESS

Trust in the Lord, and do good; dwell in the land, and feed on His faithfulness.

PSALM 37:3

LISTEN

*I*f you have been a Christian for a while, have you known anything of the faithfulness of God? Of course, you have. Do you have any reason to believe that the God who has been faithful to you in the past is going to be faithful to you in the future? Of course, you do.

One of the greatest ways you can learn to trust God is to remember and lean on His faithfulness to you in times past. As the old hymn rightly exhorts us: "Count your many blessings, name them one by one, and it will surprise you what the Lord hath done!"

Pondering God's faithful character and faithful acts toward you is like nourishment for your worried, famished soul. Doing so will sustain, strengthen, and refresh you even in the most volatile times.

Sleep on This:

Tonight, a banqueting table lies before you. Feed on God's faithfulness. Nourish your soul with remembrance of His integrity. Trust in the Lord.

80

Your Refuge

IN TROUBLE

The Lord is my rock, my fortress and my deliverer;
my God is my rock, in whom I take refuge, my shield
and the horn of my salvation, my stronghold.

PSALM 18:2, NIV

LISTEN

*T*onight's key verse proclaims that God is the rock in whom we take refuge. The Hebrew word "refuge" means a safe, quiet place to go for protection. The Old Testament mentions the "refuge" aspect of God's extraordinary character numerous times.

- Deuteronomy 33:27 says, "The eternal God is your refuge, and underneath are the everlasting arms."

- Psalm 46:1 says, "God is our refuge and strength, a very present help in trouble."

- Psalm 91:2 says, "I will say of the Lord, 'He is my refuge and my fortress; my God, in Him I will trust.'"

What a wonderful refuge we have in our gracious God!

Sleep on This:

Your Heavenly Father is your refuge in times of trouble. He is a safe place to run for protection, no matter how shaky our world grows.

81

Grace

PRODUCES PEACE

Grace to you and peace from God the Father and our Lord Jesus Christ, who gave Himself for our sins, that He might deliver us from this present evil age, according to the will of our God and Father, to whom be glory forever and ever. Amen.

GALATIANS 1:3-5

LISTEN

*Y*ou might have noticed that in Paul's letters he often opens and closes them with this little phrase: "Grace to you and peace," as he does in tonight's key verse. Notice that it is always "grace" and then "peace," never the other way around. Why? It is because when the grace of God comes to you, the result is invariably peace.

The gift of grace produces the effect of peace. And oh, what a wonderful thing this is! How grateful we should be that in this world that is so filled with turmoil and stress and conflict and upset—that we can have the peace of God. We have it because His grace is ever and always flowing toward us.

Sleep on This:

No matter how evil this present age may grow, you can enjoy an inward peace because God's grace is abundant and inexhaustible.

82

Noble and Lovely
THOUGHTS

Finally, brethren, whatever things are true, whatever things are noble, whatever things are just, whatever things are pure, whatever things are lovely, whatever things are of good report, if there is any virtue and if there is anything praiseworthy—meditate on these things.

PHILIPPIANS 4:8

LISTEN

"Garbage in, garbage out." The majority of computer programmers learn this axiom early in their training.

In tonight's key verse, Paul provides a helpful guide to programming the most sophisticated computer the planet will ever see—the human brain. He provides a profile of the kinds of thoughts on which every Christian should focus.

Paul is saying, "If you want to be free from stress and worry in your mind, take determined action to program your mind with the positive truths that are illustrated by these characteristics."

The point is, we have a choice to make. Even secular humanists, anthropologists, and scientific behaviorists understand the wisdom of what God's Word reveals here. Namely that the human being controls his or her mind and that the mind controls the human being. Garbage in, garbage out.

Sleep on This:

Tonight, let your thoughts meditate exclusively on things that are true, noble, just, pure, lovely, and of good report.

83

The End

OF PEOPLE PLEASING

The fear of man brings a snare,
but whoever trusts in the Lord shall be safe.

PROVERBS 29:25

LISTEN

$\mathcal{W}$e all have a built-in longing for approval. It is a fundamental part of being human. But what tonight's key verse calls "fear of man," describes a state in which the need for the approval of others becomes the dominant force in our life. The longing for approval is so strong that we spend our life chasing after it, often sacrificing our values and priorities in order to get it. As the verse declares, that craving for approval becomes a "snare." In other words, people pleasing is a trap.

What is the antidote to the fear of man? Proverbs 29:25 tells us the answer is found by putting our trust fully in the Lord. This theme is also mentioned in Psalm 56:11 which says, "In God I have put my trust; I will not be afraid. What can man do to me?"

Sleep on This:

You are loved and accepted by God. You can completely trust in Him. You are now free to stop focusing on pleasing people and focus on pleasing your Heavenly Father.

Financial Security

I have been young, and now am old; yet I have not seen the righteous forsaken, nor his descendants begging bread.

PSALM 37:25

LISTEN

*I*t's tempting to worry about money, but the whole issue of financial stability is an issue of trust. And here the Bible says that we can fully and wholeheartedly trust in God for our provision. You can trust in God too, and that's a decision you make. You *decide* to trust in the Lord.

The command to "trust in the Lord" appears three times in Psalm 37. On a similar note, the apostle Paul wrote: "And my God shall supply all your need according to His riches in glory by Christ Jesus" (Philippians 4:19).

Where can you find something to put your trust in that will not fail you? The psalmist tells us to trust in God. Trust is not an emotional impulse. It is not a fleeting feeling. Trust is a decision. Nothing in this material world can offer genuine security. Nothing is worthy of your trust. But God is.

Sleep on This:

Relocate the focus of your sense of security from fallible, fleeting finances to our unfailing, omnipotent God.

85

Quietness
AND CONFIDENCE

For thus says the Lord God, the Holy One of Israel:
"In returning and rest you shall be saved;
in quietness and confidence shall be
your strength." But you would not.

ISAIAH 30:15

LISTEN

*T*he context of tonight's key verse is the nation of Judah under attack from her enemies. Through the prophet Isaiah, God is graciously offering them advice on what to do under pressure or in a stressful situation.

He reminds His people that salvation comes "in returning" to Him. That strength is found in being quietly confident in Him. But note the sad last sentence: "But you would not."

We all have a human tendency to try harder when under attack by upsetting circumstances. When stress hits, instead of hitting our knees to seek God's help, the human survival instinct is to work longer, think harder, and struggle more.

Reject this impulse. Cast your cares upon your Heavenly Father tonight. For "in returning and rest you shall be saved."

Sleep on This:

Quietness and confidence are the birthrights of a child of God, even in the most perilous circumstances.

86

Heavenly
GPS

I will instruct you and teach you in the way you should go; I will guide you with My eye.

PSALM 32:8

LISTEN

We have all come to depend on the map apps on our phones and in our cars. It's a little strange to think about the time, not all that long ago, when we used paper maps and occasionally had to stop and ask for directions. Now we just ask the nice "lady" on our app to give us turn-by-turn directions.

Of course, the accuracy of those directions depends on two things. First that the "lady" knows precisely where you are. And second, that you accurately communicated your desired destination.

Here's wonderful news. The Lord Jesus has a GPS that never fails. He is never in doubt about where you currently are. In His mercy He happily meets you there. And He knows precisely where you need to go. You might take a willful detour or two along the way, but your ultimate destination is never in doubt. Never!

Sleep on This:

If you'll let Him, your Lord and Savior will guide you turn by turn, step by step, through the journey of life and will bring you safely home.

87

Your Coming

AND GOING

The Lord shall preserve you from all evil;
He shall preserve your soul.
The Lord shall preserve your going out and your coming
in from this time forth, and even forevermore.

PSALM 121:7-8

LISTEN

*L*et's break down the wonderful implications of tonight's passage. Notice that He preserves you from all evil. In other words, you are to be confident that no harm or disaster is outside of the control and the care of God. It is all filtered through His hands. He hasn't lost control when difficult things come into your life.

The Lord preserves your existence. The psalmist announces that the Lord will keep your soul from all harm, and the word "soul" is the word for life. In other words, He is going to keep your life.

These verses continue with how He preserves you every day, including your "going out and your coming in." This is a wonderful Old Testament idiom that speaks of the regular routines of life. It is also a wonderful reminder of God's watchfulness over us!

Sleep on This:

The Lord is watching over you with love and tender care. Even the smallest details of your daily routine are His concern.

— 88 —

Fret Not

*Rest in the Lord, and wait patiently for Him; do not
fret because of him who prospers in his way, because
of the man who brings wicked schemes to pass.*

PSALM 37:7

LISTEN

*A*s Christians, we are occasionally tempted to look around and say, "Lord, I'm serving You. I'm honoring You. I'm doing everything I know to do to be an obedient Christian. Why are all these people—who don't even know how to say Your Name without cursing—doing so well?"

Tonight's key verse contains heaven's response to that question: "Do not fret."

The word "fret" is an interesting word. It has two different meanings. One meaning is to "gnaw at" like a rat gnawing at a rope. The other meaning is an explosive burst of flame. Worry is like that. It is either gnawing at you or burning you up on the inside.

And so the Lord says, "When it seems life is unfair, don't fret. Exterminate the rat, put out the fire, and get on with your life." Worry will change nothing. But it will eat you up.

Sleep on This:

You are loved and cared for by God. Do not fret because of evildoers. Instead, delight yourself in the Lord.

— 89 —

Morning Joy

Weeping may endure for a night, but joy comes in the morning....
You have turned for me my mourning into dancing; You
have put off my sackcloth and clothed me with gladness.

PSALM 30:5, 11

LISTEN

A man was once asked to cite his favorite verse in the Bible, and his reply was, "And it came to pass." In other words, it didn't come to stay. It came to *pass*.

In a season of trouble, it's easy to think your circumstances are forever. When you have that thought, remember tonight's key verse. We are now in the "night" time of life. But the Bible says there is going to be a "morning" that dawns someday.

All of the sorrow and sadness and difficulty that we have known in our nighttime of life will disappear in the dawn of that new day. The Lord is going to heal every hurt, take away every sickness, and restore every blemish. Morning is coming.

Sleep on This:

Whatever you're facing tonight, it will pass. Joy comes in the morning. Just as day follows night, dancing follows mourning.

— 90 —

Take Comfort

IN GOD'S "NEVERS"

The steadfast love of the Lord never ceases;
his mercies never come to an end; they are new
every morning; great is your faithfulness.

LAMENTATIONS 3:22-23, ESV

LISTEN

There are two instances of the word "never" in tonight's key verse. That word can carry a finality about it that makes us shudder. But our Heavenly Father puts that word to good use in His Word. There He turned the word "never" into a blessed word for Christians. Consider these verses:

- "Cast your burden on the Lord, and He shall sustain you; He shall *never* permit the righteous to be moved" (Psalm 55:22, emphasis added).

- "Whoever drinks of the water that I shall give him will *never* thirst" (John 4:14, emphasis added).

- "He who comes to Me shall *never* hunger" (John 6:35, emphasis added).

- "I give them eternal life, and they shall *never* perish; neither shall anyone snatch them out of My hand" (John 10:28, emphasis added).

- "I will *never* leave you nor forsake you" (Hebrews 13:5, emphasis added).

Sleep on This:

As you close your eyes to rest, anchor your heart in the knowledge that God is faithful to all the "nevers" concerning you. His love *never* ceases. His mercies *never* end. He will *never* leave you. He will *never* forsake you.

From Overwhelmed
TO OVERJOYED

But Jesus looked at them and said to them,
"With men this is impossible, but with
God all things are possible."

MATTHEW 19:26

LISTEN

*S*ome days the demands of life feel impossible. Our days are chock-full of work obligations, family responsibilities, kitchen chores, trips to the grocery store, financial tasks, doctor appointments, church services, schoolwork, emails, texts, dishwashing, exercise, and rush-hour traffic.

If you want help with "impossible" days, you have to know the God who does the impossible. Without Christ, we're overwhelmed. With Him, we're overjoyed. We have a spiritual basis for living productively. We have a Heavenly Father who plans our life step by step.

With Him all things are possible.

Sleep on This:

As you close your eyes to end this day, ponder and meditate on the biblical truth that you belong to a God who does the impossible. Take comfort and hope from knowing that no matter what problems life may throw at you, they're not too hard for God.

—92—

He Knows

For we do not have a High Priest who cannot sympathize with our weaknesses, but was in all points tempted as we are, yet without sin. Let us therefore come boldly to the throne of grace, that we may obtain mercy and find grace to help in time of need.

HEBREWS 4:15-16

LISTEN

*N*o matter who you are or where you have been in your journey with Christ, there will inevitably come a time when you feel that nobody on earth can understand your situation. Neither your spouse, your most intimate friends, nor your family will be able to "get" what is going on in your life.

Our questions and doubts may not even be translatable into words, and we will ache for someone to whom we can go to with the needs of our soul. That's where the glory and beauty of tonight's key verse comes in.

In Jesus, you have a great High Priest who knows everything about you. He knows what you're going through. And because of Him, you can come boldly to God's throne of grace to find help.

Sleep on This:

You have a High Priest who sympathizes with your weaknesses. So come boldly to God's throne tonight. There you'll find mercy, grace, and help.

93

He Redeems

THE IRREDEEMABLE

*And we know that all things work together
for good to those who love God, to those who
are the called according to His purpose.*

ROMANS 8:28

LISTEN

$\mathcal{A}$s you look back at your life, can you remember a circumstance that happened to you which made absolutely no sense to you at the time? You could not comprehend how anything good could come out of it or how anything could be beneficial to you. A circumstance that at the time had you thinking, "God, what is this all about?"

Life in a fallen, broken world filled with broken people will inevitably bring moments like that. Which is why you will want to keep tonight's key verse close in both mind and heart.

As believers, as time passes, it's not unusual to see how God took a seemingly irredeemable event and redeemed it, using it for our good. This is more than just a verse for you tonight—it is a solemn, certain, comforting promise.

Sleep on This:

No matter what tomorrow and the days that follow hold, you can know this with great certainty: Your kind Heavenly Father will faithfully cause them to work for your good and His purpose.

94

The Secret Ingredient

Look at the birds of the air, for they neither sow nor reap nor gather into barns; yet your heavenly Father feeds them. Are you not of more value than they?

MATTHEW 6:26

LISTEN

*R*esearch has shown that 92 percent of the things people worry about never happen. That's right; 92 percent of all worry, anxiety, and fear is pointless.

We all have a choice to make. We can spend our life totally consumed with what isn't going to happen. Or we can follow the sound, wise advice of Jesus in tonight's key verse and remember how valuable we are to our Heavenly Father.

And we can pray. Paul's advice to the church in Philippi about prayer contains a secret ingredient. He said we should bring our requests to God "with thanksgiving" (Philippians 4:6). Do you fold this vital ingredient into your prayer mix? There is no better time than right now to begin doing so.

If we will bring our requests to God in thanksgiving, His incomprehensible peace will guard our heart and mind.

Sleep on This:

Reject worry tonight. Make the choice to "look at the birds of the air" and remember to "be anxious for nothing." Take your concerns to your Father, but before you do, spend a little time contemplating the many things for which you're grateful.

95

Resident

OR PRESIDENT?

*But the Helper, the Holy Spirit, whom the Father
will send in My name, He will teach you all things....
Nevertheless I tell you the truth. It is to your advantage
that I go away; for if I do not go away, the Helper will not
come to you; but if I depart, I will send Him to you.*

JOHN 14:26; 16:7

*L*ike every believer, you have the Holy Spirit within you to help you. God gave Him to you. And, as the two verses we're focusing on tonight reveal, Jesus repeatedly called Him, "the Helper."

He not only wants to be the *Resident* in your life. He wants to be the *President* of your life. When you are saved, He becomes the Resident. But there's a time when all of us get tired of trying to live life our own way and in our own power, and we elect Him President of our life. And when that happens, then come joy and peace.

Sleep on This:

The Holy Spirit, the third Member of the Godhead, lives within you. And He is ready and willing to be your Helper if you'll let Him.

96

The Lord Will

FIGHT FOR YOU

Don't be afraid. Just stand still.... The Lord himself will fight for you. Just stay calm.

EXODUS 14:13-14, NLT

LISTEN

*T*oday's key Scripture was spoken by Moses to the Israelites when they had their backs to the Red Sea and a wave of Egyptian chariots and soldiers were thundering toward them.

This is a message for us all in these chaotic times: Be reassured. Keep calm. Don't lose heart. Stand still... the Lord will fight for you. Do those words reverberate in your heart right now in light of the situation you are currently facing?

The devil may try to invade your turf. You may face battles on multiple fronts. You may live in turbulent times, but you can fix your thoughts on Jesus, claim His perfect peace, and persevere.

There is no need to be afraid. You don't have to fight your battles. No matter how grim your circumstances may seem, you can simply stand still as the Lord Himself fights for you.

Sleep on This:

Don't lose heart or be dismayed in these times of turmoil and chaos. God is on His throne, and He is mighty beyond your ability to imagine.

97

A Love

THAT NEVER QUITS

I taught Ephraim to walk, taking them by their arms; but they did not know that I healed them. I drew them with gentle cords, with bands of love, and I was to them as those who take the yoke from their neck. I stooped and fed them.

HOSEA 11:3-4

LISTEN

I am convinced from long experience that one of Satan's greatest strategies is to lie to us about the limits of God's love. Satan knows that we are fallen human beings, and we are tempted to love one another with limits. He also knows that with a little nudge, we will project our sense of worth onto how we perceive God's love.

And so rather than counting on God's unrelenting, unconditional, unending love, we will wallow in shame over our sin. And while we are feeling unloved, God is loving us. Too often, we are just not able to perceive or receive it.

That's the message of tonight's key passage. The context is God expressing His heart of love and tender care for an entire nation of people, the northern kingdom of Israel (Ephraim). He hasn't changed; He loves you as well.

Sleep on This:

God's love for you is limitless. It doesn't quit. Perceive it. Receive it. And thank Him for it.

98

Your Unbreakable

CONNECTION

Who shall separate us from the love of Christ? Shall tribulation, or distress, or persecution, or famine, or nakedness, or peril, or sword?... For I am persuaded that neither death nor life, nor angels nor principalities nor powers, nor things present nor things to come, nor height nor depth, nor any other created thing, shall be able to separate us from the love of God which is in Christ Jesus our Lord.

ROMANS 8:35, 38-39

LISTEN

*P*aul, inspired by the Holy Spirit, knew that it can sometimes appear as though we have been separated from God's love. We go through seasons in our life that make us think that God has forgotten us. Even the Old Testament writers of the book of Psalms had moments like this. David cried out, "O God, how long before you remember me? Lord God, what are you waiting for?" (See Psalm 13:1.)

In tonight's key passage, Paul asks a question in the first sentence and answers it in the final one. What can separate us from the love of Christ? The comforting answer is "nothing."

Reconnect your heart to the truth of God's Word tonight.

Sleep on This:

You are connected to infinite, perfect love. God's love. And nothing—nothing—can separate you from it.

99

The Door of Hope

I will give her her vineyards from there, and the Valley of Achor as a door of hope; she shall sing there, as in the days of her youth.

HOSEA 2:15

LISTEN

*T*onight's key verse, taken from a prophecy by Hosea, contains a reference to "the Valley of Achor." The Hebrew word translated "Achor" means "trouble."

Have you ever felt that you were living in a deep, dark valley of trouble? We all have. Perhaps you feel that way right now. In such a place, it's easy to lose hope. The good news in this verse is that no matter how deep your valley of trouble, there is always a "door of hope" in God.

The psalmist David wrote, "Why are you cast down, O my soul? And why are you disquieted within me? Hope in God" (Psalm 43:5). When we lose hope, it simply means we've lost sight of God. With Him, there is always a "door of hope."

Sleep on This:

Even in a valley of trouble, you can sing a song of hope. For God is faithful, kind, and infinitely worthy of your trust.

100

God Cares

ABOUT YOUR SLEEP

They slumber sweetly whom faith rocks to sleep.
No pillow so soft as a promise.

CHARLES HADDON SPURGEON

LISTEN

*W*e close this series of devotions with a quote rather than a Scripture. Spurgeon rightly suggests that faith is the powerful spiritual antidote to worry, anxiety, and fear. And we have filled this devotional with promises from Scripture because "no pillow [is] so soft as a promise" from God's Word.

The fact is, the Bible is filled with evidence that God cares about your sleep:

- Psalm 4:8 says, "I will both lie down in peace, and sleep; for You alone, O Lord, make me dwell in safety."

- Psalm 63:6 says, "When I remember You on my bed, I meditate on You in the night watches."

- Psalm 74:16 says, "The day is Yours, the night also is Yours; You have prepared the light and the sun."

- Psalm 127:2 says, "He gives His beloved sleep."

- Psalm 149:5 says, "Let the saints be joyful in glory; let them sing aloud on their beds."

Sleep on This:

No detail of your life is so small that it is inconsequential to God. Lay your weary, swirling head down on His promises tonight, and let faith rock you to sleep.

ENDNOTES

1. D. Martyn Lloyd-Jones, *Spiritual Depression: Its Causes and Cure* (Grand Rapids, MI: Eerdmans Publishing Company, 1965), 20-21.
2. Rob Morgan, "Speaking of Prayer," Robert J. Morgan, January 19, 2011, https://www.robertjmorgan.com/devotional/speaking-of-prayer/.
3. "Religion: Promises," *Time*, December 24, 1956, https://content.time.com/time/subscriber/article/0,33009,808851,00.html.

About the Author

Dr. David Jeremiah

· · · · · · · · · ·

David Jeremiah is the founder of Turning Point for God, an international broadcast ministry committed to providing Christians with sound Bible teaching through radio and television, the Internet, live events, and resource materials and books. He is the author of more than seventy-five books including *After the Rapture*, *The God You May Not Know*, and *Where Do We Go From Here?*. David serves as senior pastor of Shadow Mountain Community Church in San Diego, California, where he resides with his wife, Donna. They have four grown children and twelve grandchildren.

Stay Connected to David Jeremiah

. . . .

Turning Points Magazine and Devotional

Receive Dr. Jeremiah's magazine,
Turning Points, each month:

- Thematic study focus
- 52 pages of life-changing reading
- Relevant articles
- Daily devotional readings and more!

Request *Turning Points* magazine today!
(800) 947-1993 | DavidJeremiah.org/Magazine

Daily Turning Point E-Devotional

Receive a daily e-devotion from Dr. Jeremiah
that will strengthen your walk with God and
encourage you to live the authentic Christian life

Sign up for your free e-devotional today!
www.DavidJeremiah.org/Devo

Turning Point Mobile App

Access Dr. Jeremiah's video teachings, audio
sermons, and more wherever you are!

Download your free app today!
www.DavidJeremiah.org/App

The Jeremiah Study Bible

· · · · · · · · · · ·

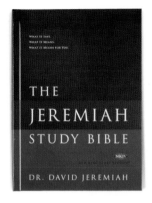

WHAT THE BIBLE SAYS.
WHAT IT MEANS.
WHAT IT MEANS FOR YOU.

The Jeremiah Study Bible is comprehensive, yet easy to understand. More than forty years in the making, it is deeply personal and designed to transform your life. No matter your place or time in history, Scripture always speaks to the important issues of life. Hear God speak to you through studying His Word in *The Jeremiah Study Bible*.

Now available in:

- New Kings James Version • Large Print
- New International Version • English Standard Version

Additional Resources
from David Jeremiah

· · · · · · · · · · ·

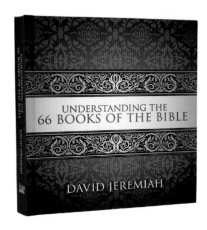

UNDERSTANDING THE 66 BOOKS OF THE BIBLE
Understanding the 66 Books of the Bible is a resource to orient
you to each of God's special books whether you're a new
reader or a veteran student, whether you want to visit the
Gospel of John or take a journey into Nahum or Jude. In this
volume by Dr. Jeremiah, you'll find a simple digest for each of
the 66 books—Genesis to Revelation. After all, God's Word is
a big book. It will be the fastest journey through the Bible you
will ever experience!

Find this resource at DavidJeremiah.org

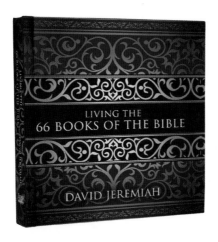

LIVING THE 66 BOOKS OF THE BIBLE

It's one thing to understand the 66 books of the Bible. It's another thing to live them, to put them into practice, and to be doers of the Word. Nothing can touch your life and touch this world so deeply as living the 66 books of the Bible. In *Living the 66 Books of the Bible*, Dr. Jeremiah identifies each book's purpose, theme, challenge, verse, and prayer. You will find insights and applications to help you live out Scripture in your daily life.

Find this resource at DavidJeremiah.org

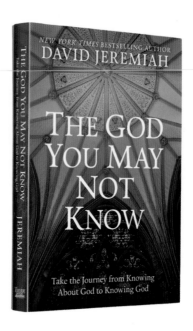

THE GOD YOU MAY NOT KNOW

We as Christians often think knowing about God is enough, but the truth is, in order to love God, we must know Him in a personal way, immersing ourselves in the study of God and His incredible attributes. In *The God You May Not Know*, Dr. Jeremiah introduces you to the God you may not know—to His knowledge, holiness, all-pervasive presence, unlimited power, love, and the other qualities that make Him who He is. Knowing our eternal God changes our daily lives—and He is well worth knowing, for He alone is worthy of all praise!

Find this resource at DavidJeremiah.org

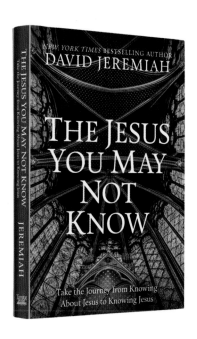

THE JESUS YOU MAY NOT KNOW

In *The Jesus You May Not Know*, Dr. Jeremiah answers probing questions about Jesus including: Is He From History or From Eternity? Is He the Teacher of Truth or the Truth to be Taught? Is He Praying for Us or Are We Praying to Him? Jesus is the mystery of the ages and the marvel of history. But He is also personable and knowable. Through this book, you will learn more about Him—the One who longs for your fellowship.

PRAYERS & THOUGHTS

PRAYERS & THOUGHTS

PRAYERS & THOUGHTS